Technology Evaluation
Complete Self-Assessment Guide

C000151524

The guidance in this Self-Assessment is based on
best practices and standards in business process ...., design
and quality management. The guidance is also based on the professional
judgment of the individual collaborators listed in the Acknowledgments.

Notice of rights

**You are licensed to use the Self-Assessment contents in your
presentations and materials for internal use and customers
without asking us - we are here to help.**

All rights reserved for the book itself: this book may not be reproduced
or transmitted in any form by any means, electronic, mechanical,
photocopying, recording, or otherwise, without the prior written
permission of the publisher.

The information in this book is distributed on an "As Is" basis without
warranty. While every precaution has been taken in the preparation of he
book, neither the author nor the publisher shall have any liability to any
person or entity with respect to any loss or damage caused or alleged to
be caused directly or indirectly by the instructions contained in this book
or by the products described in it.

Trademarks

Many of the designations used by manufacturers and sellers to
distinguish their products are claimed as trademarks. Where those
designations appear in this book, and the publisher was aware of a
trademark claim, the designations appear as requested by the owner
of the trademark. All other product names and services identified
throughout this book are used in editorial fashion only and for the
benefit of such companies with no intention of infringement of the
trademark. No such use, or the use of any trade name, is intended to
convey endorsement or other affiliation with this book.

Copyright © by The Art of Service
http://theartofservice.com
service@theartofservice.com

Table of Contents

About The Art of Service

The Art of Service, Business Process Architects since 2000, is dedicated to helping stakeholders achieve excellence.

Defining, designing, creating, and implementing a process to solve a stakeholders challenge or meet an objective is the most valuable role… In EVERY group, company, organization and department.

Unless you're talking a one-time, single-use project, there should be a process. Whether that process is managed and implemented by humans, AI, or a combination of the two, it needs to be designed by someone with a complex enough perspective to ask the right questions.

Someone capable of asking the right questions and step back and say, 'What are we really trying to accomplish here? And is there a different way to look at it?'

With The Art of Service's Standard Requirements Self-Assessments, we empower people who can do just that — whether their title is marketer, entrepreneur, manager, salesperson, consultant, Business Process Manager, executive assistant, IT Manager, CIO etc... —they are the people who rule the future. They are people who watch the process as it happens, and ask the right questions to make the process work better.

Contact us when you need any support with this Self-Assessment and any help with templates, blue-prints and examples of standard documents you might need:

http://theartofservice.com
service@theartofservice.com

Included Resources - how to access

Included with your purchase of the book is the Technology

Evaluation Self-Assessment Spreadsheet Dashboard which contains all questions and Self-Assessment areas and auto-generates insights, graphs, and project RACI planning - all with examples to get you started right away.

How? Simply send an email to
access@theartofservice.com
with this books' title in the subject to get the Technology Evaluation Self Assessment Tool right away.

You will receive the following contents with New and Updated specific criteria:

- The latest quick edition of the book in PDF

- The latest complete edition of the book in PDF, which criteria correspond to the criteria in...

- The Self-Assessment Excel Dashboard, and...

- Example pre-filled Self-Assessment Excel Dashboard to get familiar with results generation

- In-depth specific Checklists covering the topic

- Project management checklists and templates to assist with implementation

INCLUDES LIFETIME SELF ASSESSMENT UPDATES

Every self assessment comes with Lifetime Updates and Lifetime Free Updated Books. Lifetime Updates is an industry-first feature which allows you to receive verified self assessment updates, ensuring you always have the most accurate information at your fingertips.

Get it now- you will be glad you did - do it now, before you forget.

Send an email to **access@theartofservice.com** with this books' title in the subject to get the Technology Evaluation Self Assessment Tool right away.

Purpose of this Self-Assessment

This Self-Assessment has been developed to improve understanding of the requirements and elements of Technology Evaluation, based on best practices and standards in business process architecture, design and quality management.

It is designed to allow for a rapid Self-Assessment to determine how closely existing management practices and procedures correspond to the elements of the Self-Assessment.

The criteria of requirements and elements of Technology Evaluation have been rephrased in the format of a Self-Assessment questionnaire, with a seven-criterion scoring system, as explained in this document.

In this format, even with limited background knowledge of Technology Evaluation, a manager can quickly review existing operations to determine how they measure up to the standards. This in turn can serve as the starting point of a 'gap analysis' to identify management tools or system elements that might usefully be implemented in the organization to help improve overall performance.

How to use the Self-Assessment

On the following pages are a series of questions to identify to what extent your Technology Evaluation initiative is complete in comparison to the requirements set in standards.

To facilitate answering the questions, there is a space in front of each question to enter a score on a scale of '1' to '5'.

1 Strongly Disagree

2 Disagree

3 Neutral

4 Agree

5 Strongly Agree

Read the question and rate it with the following in front of mind:

**'In my belief,
the answer to this question is clearly defined'.**

There are two ways in which you can choose to interpret this statement;
1. how aware are you that the answer to the question is clearly defined
2. for more in-depth analysis you can choose to gather evidence and confirm the answer to the question. This obviously will take more time, most Self-Assessment users opt for the first way to interpret the question and dig deeper later on based on the outcome of the overall Self-Assessment.

A score of '1' would mean that the answer is not clear at all, where a '5' would mean the answer is crystal clear and defined. Leave emtpy when the question is not applicable or you don't want to answer it, you can skip it without affecting your score. Write your score in the space provided.

After you have responded to all the appropriate statements in each section, compute your average score for that section, using the formula provided, and round to the nearest tenth. Then transfer to the corresponding spoke in the Technology Evaluation Scorecard on the second next page of the Self-Assessment.

Your completed Technology Evaluation Scorecard will give you a clear presentation of which Technology Evaluation areas need attention.

Technology Evaluation Scorecard Example

Example of how the finalized Scorecard can look like:

Technology Evaluation Scorecard

Your Scores:

BEGINNING OF THE SELF-ASSESSMENT:

CRITERION #1: RECOGNIZE

INTENT: Be aware of the need for change. Recognize that there is an unfavorable variation, problem or symptom.

In my belief, the answer to this question is clearly defined:

5 Strongly Agree

4 Agree

3 Neutral

2 Disagree

1 Strongly Disagree

1. What training and capacity building actions are needed to implement proposed reforms?
<--- Score

2. What are the technology evaluation resources needed?
<--- Score

3. Which issues are too important to ignore?

<--- Score

4. For your technology evaluation project, identify and describe the business environment, is there more than one layer to the business environment?
<--- Score

5. Whom do you really need or want to serve?
<--- Score

6. What technology evaluation capabilities do you need?
<--- Score

7. Will new equipment/products be required to facilitate technology evaluation delivery, for example is new software needed?
<--- Score

8. Do you have/need 24-hour access to key personnel?
<--- Score

9. Does the problem have ethical dimensions?
<--- Score

10. Would you recognize a threat from the inside?
<--- Score

11. Who are your key stakeholders who need to sign off?
<--- Score

12. How are you going to measure success?
<--- Score

13. What extra resources will you need?
<--- Score

14. Do you know what you need to know about technology evaluation?
<--- Score

15. Who else hopes to benefit from it?
<--- Score

16. Who needs to know?
<--- Score

17. Is the quality assurance team identified?
<--- Score

18. Is it needed?
<--- Score

19. To what extent does each concerned units management team recognize technology evaluation as an effective investment?
<--- Score

20. Who defines the rules in relation to any given issue?
<--- Score

21. Can management personnel recognize the monetary benefit of technology evaluation?
<--- Score

22. Are your goals realistic? Do you need to redefine your problem? Perhaps the problem has changed or maybe you have reached your goal and need to set a new one?

<--- Score

23. What are the clients issues and concerns?
<--- Score

24. What creative shifts do you need to take?
<--- Score

25. What is the extent or complexity of the technology evaluation problem?
<--- Score

26. What is the technology evaluation problem definition? What do you need to resolve?
<--- Score

27. How does it fit into your organizational needs and tasks?
<--- Score

28. What are the expected benefits of technology evaluation to the stakeholder?
<--- Score

29. Will a response program recognize when a crisis occurs and provide some level of response?
<--- Score

30. Who needs budgets?
<--- Score

31. How are training requirements identified?
<--- Score

32. Are controls defined to recognize and contain problems?

<--- Score

33. Is it clear when you think of the day ahead of you what activities and tasks you need to complete?
<--- Score

34. Does your organization need more technology evaluation education?
<--- Score

35. What needs to be done?
<--- Score

36. What would happen if technology evaluation weren't done?
<--- Score

37. What technology evaluation problem should be solved?
<--- Score

38. What are your needs in relation to technology evaluation skills, labor, equipment, and markets?
<--- Score

39. What are the minority interests and what amount of minority interests can be recognized?
<--- Score

40. To what extent would your organization benefit from being recognized as a award recipient?
<--- Score

41. Are you dealing with any of the same issues today as yesterday? What can you do about this?
<--- Score

42. Are losses recognized in a timely manner?
<--- Score

43. What else needs to be measured?
<--- Score

44. Will it solve real problems?
<--- Score

45. What do employees need in the short term?
<--- Score

46. Are problem definition and motivation clearly presented?
<--- Score

47. As a sponsor, customer or management, how important is it to meet goals, objectives?
<--- Score

48. What situation(s) led to this technology evaluation Self Assessment?
<--- Score

49. What is the recognized need?
<--- Score

50. What tools and technologies are needed for a custom technology evaluation project?
<--- Score

51. What is the problem and/or vulnerability?
<--- Score

52. Are employees recognized or rewarded for

performance that demonstrates the highest levels of integrity?
<--- Score

53. What needs to stay?
<--- Score

54. How do you recognize an objection?
<--- Score

55. Are there regulatory / compliance issues?
<--- Score

56. Are there technology evaluation problems defined?
<--- Score

57. Who needs what information?
<--- Score

58. What are the stakeholder objectives to be achieved with technology evaluation?
<--- Score

59. Do you need different information or graphics?
<--- Score

60. How do you recognize an technology evaluation objection?
<--- Score

61. What are the timeframes required to resolve each of the issues/problems?
<--- Score

62. What technology evaluation events should you

attend?

<--- Score

63. What technology evaluation coordination do you need?

<--- Score

64. How do you identify the kinds of information that you will need?

<--- Score

65. Are there any specific expectations or concerns about the technology evaluation team, technology evaluation itself?

<--- Score

66. How much are sponsors, customers, partners, stakeholders involved in technology evaluation? In other words, what are the risks, if technology evaluation does not deliver successfully?

<--- Score

67. How are the technology evaluation's objectives aligned to the group's overall stakeholder strategy?

<--- Score

68. Who needs to know about technology evaluation?

<--- Score

69. When a technology evaluation manager recognizes a problem, what options are available?

<--- Score

70. What problems are you facing and how do you consider technology evaluation will circumvent those obstacles?

<--- Score

71. What do you need to start doing?
<--- Score

72. What prevents you from making the changes you know will make you a more effective technology evaluation leader?
<--- Score

73. What vendors make products that address the technology evaluation needs?
<--- Score

74. Are employees recognized for desired behaviors?
<--- Score

75. What should be considered when identifying available resources, constraints, and deadlines?
<--- Score

76. Think about the people you identified for your technology evaluation project and the project responsibilities you would assign to them, what kind of training do you think they would need to perform these responsibilities effectively?
<--- Score

77. Are there recognized technology evaluation problems?
<--- Score

78. Why the need?
<--- Score

79. Where is training needed?

<--- Score

80. Do you recognize technology evaluation achievements?
<--- Score

81. Why is this needed?
<--- Score

82. How can auditing be a preventative security measure?
<--- Score

83. How many trainings, in total, are needed?
<--- Score

84. Are there any revenue recognition issues?
<--- Score

85. Do you need to avoid or amend any technology evaluation activities?
<--- Score

86. Looking at each person individually – does every one have the qualities which are needed to work in this group?
<--- Score

87. Have you identified your technology evaluation key performance indicators?
<--- Score

88. What does technology evaluation success mean to the stakeholders?
<--- Score

89. What resources or support might you need?
<--- Score

90. Did you miss any major technology evaluation issues?
<--- Score

91. Where do you need to exercise leadership?
<--- Score

92. Will technology evaluation deliverables need to be tested and, if so, by whom?
<--- Score

93. Is the need for organizational change recognized?
<--- Score

94. Consider your own technology evaluation project, what types of organizational problems do you think might be causing or affecting your problem, based on the work done so far?
<--- Score

Add up total points for this section:
_ _ _ _ _ = Total points for this section

Divided by: _ _ _ _ _ _ (number of statements answered) = _ _ _ _ _ _
Average score for this section

Transfer your score to the technology evaluation Index at the beginning of the Self-Assessment.

CRITERION #2: DEFINE:

INTENT: Formulate the stakeholder problem. Define the problem, needs and objectives.

In my belief, the answer to this question is clearly defined:

5 Strongly Agree

4 Agree

3 Neutral

2 Disagree

1 Strongly Disagree

1. How would you define the culture at your organization, how susceptible is it to technology evaluation changes?
<--- Score

2. How often are the team meetings?
<--- Score

3. Is special technology evaluation user knowledge

required?

<--- Score

4. Has a high-level 'as is' process map been completed, verified and validated?

<--- Score

5. What scope to assess?

<--- Score

6. Are audit criteria, scope, frequency and methods defined?

<--- Score

7. How do you gather the stories?

<--- Score

8. Is the improvement team aware of the different versions of a process: what they think it is vs. what it actually is vs. what it should be vs. what it could be?

<--- Score

9. What baselines are required to be defined and managed?

<--- Score

10. Do you all define technology evaluation in the same way?

<--- Score

11. How do you think the partners involved in technology evaluation would have defined success?

<--- Score

12. How do you build the right business case?

<--- Score

13. When are meeting minutes sent out? Who is on the distribution list?
<--- Score

14. How do you manage scope?
<--- Score

15. What technology evaluation requirements should be gathered?
<--- Score

16. Are all requirements met?
<--- Score

17. What is the context?
<--- Score

18. Is it clearly defined in and to your organization what you do?
<--- Score

19. Have all of the relationships been defined properly?
<--- Score

20. Has everyone on the team, including the team leaders, been properly trained?
<--- Score

21. Are different versions of process maps needed to account for the different types of inputs?
<--- Score

22. How do you keep key subject matter experts in

the loop?
<--- Score

23. Does the team have regular meetings?
<--- Score

24. When is/was the technology evaluation start date?
<--- Score

25. What is out-of-scope initially?
<--- Score

26. What are the record-keeping requirements of technology evaluation activities?
<--- Score

27. How do you catch technology evaluation definition inconsistencies?
<--- Score

28. What information should you gather?
<--- Score

29. Is there a technology evaluation management charter, including stakeholder case, problem and goal statements, scope, milestones, roles and responsibilities, communication plan?
<--- Score

30. What are the compelling stakeholder reasons for embarking on technology evaluation?
<--- Score

31. Are there any constraints known that bear on the ability to perform technology evaluation work? How is the team addressing them?

<--- Score

32. What are the technology evaluation tasks and definitions?
<--- Score

33. How do you manage unclear technology evaluation requirements?
<--- Score

34. Are the technology evaluation requirements complete?
<--- Score

35. What is the worst case scenario?
<--- Score

36. How will the technology evaluation team and the group measure complete success of technology evaluation?
<--- Score

37. Is there a critical path to deliver technology evaluation results?
<--- Score

38. Are the technology evaluation requirements testable?
<--- Score

39. Have the customer needs been translated into specific, measurable requirements? How?
<--- Score

40. Are approval levels defined for contracts and supplements to contracts?

<--- Score

41. What technology evaluation services do you require?
<--- Score

42. What are the core elements of the technology evaluation business case?
<--- Score

43. Is there regularly 100% attendance at the team meetings? If not, have appointed substitutes attended to preserve cross-functionality and full representation?
<--- Score

44. How would you define technology evaluation leadership?
<--- Score

45. How do you hand over technology evaluation context?
<--- Score

46. Have all basic functions of technology evaluation been defined?
<--- Score

47. What are the Roles and Responsibilities for each team member and its leadership? Where is this documented?
<--- Score

48. What is the scope of the technology evaluation effort?
<--- Score

49. What are the technology evaluation use cases?
<--- Score

50. Why are you doing technology evaluation and what is the scope?
<--- Score

51. What system do you use for gathering technology evaluation information?
<--- Score

52. What specifically is the problem? Where does it occur? When does it occur? What is its extent?
<--- Score

53. What scope do you want your strategy to cover?
<--- Score

54. Is the current 'as is' process being followed? If not, what are the discrepancies?
<--- Score

55. Has a team charter been developed and communicated?
<--- Score

56. Is the technology evaluation scope complete and appropriately sized?
<--- Score

57. What happens if technology evaluation's scope changes?
<--- Score

58. What gets examined?

<--- Score

59. Are task requirements clearly defined?
<--- Score

60. Will a technology evaluation production readiness review be required?
<--- Score

61. What is out of scope?
<--- Score

62. Do you have a technology evaluation success story or case study ready to tell and share?
<--- Score

63. What information do you gather?
<--- Score

64. What is in the scope and what is not in scope?
<--- Score

65. Is the scope of technology evaluation defined?
<--- Score

66. What is in scope?
<--- Score

67. What are the tasks and definitions?
<--- Score

68. How do you gather technology evaluation requirements?
<--- Score

69. Is the technology evaluation scope manageable?

<--- Score

70. Is technology evaluation linked to key stakeholder goals and objectives?
<--- Score

71. How was the 'as is' process map developed, reviewed, verified and validated?
<--- Score

72. What sources do you use to gather information for a technology evaluation study?
<--- Score

73. Are there different segments of customers?
<--- Score

74. How and when will the baselines be defined?
<--- Score

75. Is data collected and displayed to better understand customer(s) critical needs and requirements.
<--- Score

76. What is the definition of technology evaluation excellence?
<--- Score

77. Has the direction changed at all during the course of technology evaluation? If so, when did it change and why?
<--- Score

78. Has the improvement team collected the 'voice of the customer' (obtained feedback – qualitative and

quantitative)?
<--- Score

79. Who approved the technology evaluation scope?
<--- Score

80. How are consistent technology evaluation definitions important?
<--- Score

81. Who is gathering information?
<--- Score

82. Has your scope been defined?
<--- Score

83. Has a project plan, Gantt chart, or similar been developed/completed?
<--- Score

84. How will variation in the actual durations of each activity be dealt with to ensure that the expected technology evaluation results are met?
<--- Score

85. How does the technology evaluation manager ensure against scope creep?
<--- Score

86. If substitutes have been appointed, have they been briefed on the technology evaluation goals and received regular communications as to the progress to date?
<--- Score

87. Has/have the customer(s) been identified?

<--- Score

88. What is a worst-case scenario for losses?
<--- Score

89. Are accountability and ownership for technology evaluation clearly defined?
<--- Score

90. Are required metrics defined, what are they?
<--- Score

91. Is technology evaluation currently on schedule according to the plan?
<--- Score

92. Have specific policy objectives been defined?
<--- Score

93. What are the dynamics of the communication plan?
<--- Score

94. The political context: who holds power?
<--- Score

95. How is the team tracking and documenting its work?
<--- Score

96. What are the rough order estimates on cost savings/opportunities that technology evaluation brings?
<--- Score

97. What is the scope of technology evaluation?

<--- Score

98. Do you have organizational privacy requirements?
<--- Score

99. What would be the goal or target for a technology evaluation's improvement team?
<--- Score

100. Does the scope remain the same?
<--- Score

101. Is there any additional technology evaluation definition of success?
<--- Score

102. What critical content must be communicated – who, what, when, where, and how?
<--- Score

103. Is there a clear technology evaluation case definition?
<--- Score

104. What is the definition of success?
<--- Score

105. What are the requirements for audit information?
<--- Score

106. Scope of sensitive information?
<--- Score

107. How do you manage changes in technology evaluation requirements?

<--- Score

108. Who defines (or who defined) the rules and roles?

<--- Score

109. What intelligence can you gather?
<--- Score

110. Who is gathering technology evaluation information?
<--- Score

111. What is the scope of the technology evaluation work?

<--- Score

112. Who are the technology evaluation improvement team members, including Management Leads and Coaches?
<--- Score

113. How can the value of technology evaluation be defined?

<--- Score

114. What key stakeholder process output measure(s) does technology evaluation leverage and how?
<--- Score

115. Is technology evaluation required?
<--- Score

116. What are the boundaries of the scope? What is in bounds and what is not? What is the start point? What is the stop point?

<--- Score

117. What constraints exist that might impact the team?
<--- Score

118. Has anyone else (internal or external to the group) attempted to solve this problem or a similar one before? If so, what knowledge can be leveraged from these previous efforts?
<--- Score

119. Has the technology evaluation work been fairly and/or equitably divided and delegated among team members who are qualified and capable to perform the work? Has everyone contributed?
<--- Score

120. Is the work to date meeting requirements?
<--- Score

121. Has a technology evaluation requirement not been met?
<--- Score

122. How did the technology evaluation manager receive input to the development of a technology evaluation improvement plan and the estimated completion dates/times of each activity?
<--- Score

123. What sort of initial information to gather?
<--- Score

124. Are resources adequate for the scope?
<--- Score

125. How do you gather requirements?
<--- Score

126. Is there a completed, verified, and validated high-level 'as is' (not 'should be' or 'could be') stakeholder process map?
<--- Score

127. Are roles and responsibilities formally defined?
<--- Score

128. Where can you gather more information?
<--- Score

129. Is the team adequately staffed with the desired cross-functionality? If not, what additional resources are available to the team?
<--- Score

130. What defines best in class?
<--- Score

131. When is the estimated completion date?
<--- Score

132. What customer feedback methods were used to solicit their input?
<--- Score

133. Do the problem and goal statements meet the SMART criteria (specific, measurable, attainable, relevant, and time-bound)?
<--- Score

134. Is there a completed SIPOC representation,

describing the Suppliers, Inputs, Process, Outputs, and
Customers?
<--- Score

Add up total points for this section:
_____ = Total points for this section

Divided by: _____ (number of
statements answered) = _____
Average score for this section

Transfer your score to the technology
evaluation Index at the beginning of
the Self-Assessment.

CRITERION #3: MEASURE:

INTENT: Gather the correct data. Measure the current performance and evolution of the situation.

In my belief, the answer to this question is clearly defined:

5 Strongly Agree

4 Agree

3 Neutral

2 Disagree

1 Strongly Disagree

1. Why do you expend time and effort to implement measurement, for whom?
<--- Score

2. Is the solution cost-effective?
<--- Score

3. How can you measure the performance?
<--- Score

4. Will technology evaluation have an impact on current business continuity, disaster recovery processes and/or infrastructure?
<--- Score

5. What drives O&M cost?
<--- Score

6. How frequently do you track technology evaluation measures?
<--- Score

7. Are the technology evaluation benefits worth its costs?
<--- Score

8. What do people want to verify?
<--- Score

9. Are you aware of what could cause a problem?
<--- Score

10. What would it cost to replace your technology?
<--- Score

11. Do you verify that corrective actions were taken?
<--- Score

12. How will costs be allocated?
<--- Score

13. Where is it measured?
<--- Score

14. How do you quantify and qualify impacts?

<--- Score

15. Who is involved in verifying compliance?
<--- Score

16. What tests verify requirements?
<--- Score

17. How is the value delivered by technology evaluation being measured?
<--- Score

18. What are your key technology evaluation organizational performance measures, including key short and longer-term financial measures?
<--- Score

19. What could cause you to change course?
<--- Score

20. Are the units of measure consistent?
<--- Score

21. How sensitive must the technology evaluation strategy be to cost?
<--- Score

22. Does a technology evaluation quantification method exist?
<--- Score

23. What are allowable costs?
<--- Score

24. Was a business case (cost/benefit) developed?
<--- Score

25. What does verifying compliance entail?
<--- Score

26. Are you able to realize any cost savings?
<--- Score

27. Among the technology evaluation product and service cost to be estimated, which is considered hardest to estimate?
<--- Score

28. When should you bother with diagrams?
<--- Score

29. Have you made assumptions about the shape of the future, particularly its impact on your customers and competitors?
<--- Score

30. Has a cost center been established?
<--- Score

31. Have design-to-cost goals been established?
<--- Score

32. What is the total cost related to deploying technology evaluation, including any consulting or professional services?
<--- Score

33. How can you reduce the costs of obtaining inputs?
<--- Score

34. When a disaster occurs, who gets priority?
<--- Score

35. What are your customers expectations and measures?

<--- Score

36. How do you verify the technology evaluation requirements quality?

<--- Score

37. What are the estimated costs of proposed changes?

<--- Score

38. Did you tackle the cause or the symptom?

<--- Score

39. What relevant entities could be measured?

<--- Score

40. What is your decision requirements diagram?

<--- Score

41. What are the operational costs after technology evaluation deployment?

<--- Score

42. Do you have a flow diagram of what happens?

<--- Score

43. Are you taking your company in the direction of better and revenue or cheaper and cost?

<--- Score

44. How do you measure success?

<--- Score

45. How will your organization measure success?
<--- Score

46. How do you aggregate measures across priorities?
<--- Score

47. What are your operating costs?
<--- Score

48. What does a Test Case verify?
<--- Score

49. How will success or failure be measured?
<--- Score

50. How do you measure variability?
<--- Score

51. How is progress measured?
<--- Score

52. What measurements are possible, practicable and meaningful?
<--- Score

53. What disadvantage does this cause for the user?
<--- Score

54. How do you measure efficient delivery of technology evaluation services?
<--- Score

55. Are the measurements objective?
<--- Score

56. What are the technology evaluation investment

costs?
<--- Score

57. Do the benefits outweigh the costs?
<--- Score

58. How do you verify if technology evaluation is built right?
<--- Score

59. How do you control the overall costs of your work processes?
<--- Score

60. What could cause delays in the schedule?
<--- Score

61. What are the strategic priorities for this year?
<--- Score

62. Do you have any cost technology evaluation limitation requirements?
<--- Score

63. Do you aggressively reward and promote the people who have the biggest impact on creating excellent technology evaluation services/ products?
<--- Score

64. Is there an opportunity to verify requirements?
<--- Score

65. Which costs should be taken into account?
<--- Score

66. What are the uncertainties surrounding estimates of impact?

<--- Score

67. Why do the measurements/indicators matter?

<--- Score

68. How will you measure your technology evaluation effectiveness?

<--- Score

69. What is your technology evaluation quality cost segregation study?

<--- Score

70. Do you have an issue in getting priority?

<--- Score

71. What would be a real cause for concern?

<--- Score

72. Do you effectively measure and reward individual and team performance?

<--- Score

73. What is the technology evaluation business impact?

<--- Score

74. How can you manage cost down?

<--- Score

75. Have you included everything in your technology evaluation cost models?

<--- Score

76. Which technology evaluation impacts are significant?

<--- Score

77. How will measures be used to manage and adapt?

<--- Score

78. What happens if cost savings do not materialize?

<--- Score

79. Are technology evaluation vulnerabilities categorized and prioritized?

<--- Score

80. What are the costs of delaying technology evaluation action?

<--- Score

81. How much does it cost?

<--- Score

82. Is it possible to estimate the impact of unanticipated complexity such as wrong or failed assumptions, feedback, etcetera on proposed reforms?

<--- Score

83. Who should receive measurement reports?

<--- Score

84. What causes innovation to fail or succeed in your organization?

<--- Score

85. How do you verify the authenticity of the data and

information used?

<--- Score

86. How to cause the change?

<--- Score

87. What are your primary costs, revenues, assets?

<--- Score

88. What users will be impacted?

<--- Score

89. What evidence is there and what is measured?

<--- Score

90. What causes investor action?

<--- Score

91. Are missed technology evaluation opportunities costing your organization money?

<--- Score

92. What does your operating model cost?

<--- Score

93. What is the cause of any technology evaluation gaps?

<--- Score

94. How do you verify and validate the technology evaluation data?

<--- Score

95. Are there competing technology evaluation priorities?

<--- Score

96. Are supply costs steady or fluctuating?
<--- Score

97. What are the types and number of measures to use?
<--- Score

98. What is an unallowable cost?
<--- Score

99. What causes extra work or rework?
<--- Score

100. Are there any easy-to-implement alternatives to technology evaluation? Sometimes other solutions are available that do not require the cost implications of a full-blown project?
<--- Score

101. What harm might be caused?
<--- Score

102. Which measures and indicators matter?
<--- Score

103. Who pays the cost?
<--- Score

104. Are actual costs in line with budgeted costs?
<--- Score

105. Where is the cost?
<--- Score

106. What are the costs of reform?

<--- Score

107. What methods are feasible and acceptable to estimate the impact of reforms?
<--- Score

108. How long to keep data and how to manage retention costs?
<--- Score

109. What do you measure and why?
<--- Score

110. How can a technology evaluation test verify your ideas or assumptions?
<--- Score

111. What are the costs and benefits?
<--- Score

112. How do you verify performance?
<--- Score

113. What can be used to verify compliance?
<--- Score

114. What measurements are being captured?
<--- Score

115. How will you measure success?
<--- Score

116. When are costs are incurred?
<--- Score

117. At what cost?

<--- Score

118. Are indirect costs charged to the technology evaluation program?
<--- Score

119. What are the technology evaluation key cost drivers?
<--- Score

120. How are measurements made?
<--- Score

121. What are the current costs of the technology evaluation process?
<--- Score

122. What potential environmental factors impact the technology evaluation effort?
<--- Score

123. What details are required of the technology evaluation cost structure?
<--- Score

124. Where can you go to verify the info?
<--- Score

125. Is the cost worth the technology evaluation effort ?
<--- Score

126. What are the costs?
<--- Score

127. What are hidden technology evaluation quality

costs?

<--- Score

128. How is performance measured?

<--- Score

129. What are you verifying?

<--- Score

130. How are costs allocated?

<--- Score

131. How do you measure lifecycle phases?

<--- Score

132. How do your measurements capture actionable technology evaluation information for use in exceeding your customers expectations and securing your customers engagement?

<--- Score

133. How do you verify your resources?

<--- Score

134. How can you reduce costs?

<--- Score

135. What is the cost of rework?

<--- Score

136. How do you verify and develop ideas and innovations?

<--- Score

137. Are there measurements based on task performance?

<--- Score

138. Does the technology evaluation task fit the client's priorities?
<--- Score

139. What does losing customers cost your organization?
<--- Score

Add up total points for this section:
_ _ _ _ _   = Total points for this section

Divided by: _ _ _ _ _ _ (number of statements answered) = _ _ _ _ _ _
Average score for this section

Transfer your score to the technology evaluation Index at the beginning of the Self-Assessment.

CRITERION #4: ANALYZE:

INTENT: Analyze causes, assumptions and hypotheses.

In my belief, the answer to this question is clearly defined:

5 Strongly Agree

4 Agree

3 Neutral

2 Disagree

1 Strongly Disagree

1. What systems/processes must you excel at?
<--- Score

2. Is data and process analysis, root cause analysis and quantifying the gap/opportunity in place?
<--- Score

3. Do your contracts/agreements contain data security obligations?
<--- Score

4. What qualifications do technology evaluation leaders need?
<--- Score

5. What successful thing are you doing today that may be blinding you to new growth opportunities?
<--- Score

6. What is your organizations system for selecting qualified vendors?
<--- Score

7. How do you measure the operational performance of your key work systems and processes, including productivity, cycle time, and other appropriate measures of process effectiveness, efficiency, and innovation?
<--- Score

8. How does the organization define, manage, and improve its technology evaluation processes?
<--- Score

9. What were the crucial 'moments of truth' on the process map?
<--- Score

10. What are your technology evaluation processes?
<--- Score

11. What is the complexity of the output produced?
<--- Score

12. Is the performance gap determined?

<--- Score

13. Is the suppliers process defined and controlled?
<--- Score

14. How are outputs preserved and protected?
<--- Score

15. Is the technology evaluation process severely broken such that a re-design is necessary?
<--- Score

16. What does the data say about the performance of the stakeholder process?
<--- Score

17. What are the technology evaluation design outputs?
<--- Score

18. What is the technology evaluation Driver?
<--- Score

19. Was a cause-and-effect diagram used to explore the different types of causes (or sources of variation)?
<--- Score

20. How do you implement and manage your work processes to ensure that they meet design requirements?
<--- Score

21. How often will data be collected for measures?
<--- Score

22. Have the problem and goal statements been

updated to reflect the additional knowledge gained from the analyze phase?

<--- Score

23. What are your current levels and trends in key measures or indicators of technology evaluation product and process performance that are important to and directly serve your customers? How do these results compare with the performance of your competitors and other organizations with similar offerings?

<--- Score

24. What types of data do your technology evaluation indicators require?

<--- Score

25. Was a detailed process map created to amplify critical steps of the 'as is' stakeholder process?

<--- Score

26. What output to create?

<--- Score

27. How do you promote understanding that opportunity for improvement is not criticism of the status quo, or the people who created the status quo?

<--- Score

28. What is the cost of poor quality as supported by the team's analysis?

<--- Score

29. Do several people in different organizational units assist with the technology evaluation process?

<--- Score

30. Record-keeping requirements flow from the records needed as inputs, outputs, controls and for transformation of a technology evaluation process, are the records needed as inputs to the technology evaluation process available?
<--- Score

31. What process should you select for improvement?
<--- Score

32. What do you need to qualify?
<--- Score

33. How is data used for program management and improvement?
<--- Score

34. Who qualifies to gain access to data?
<--- Score

35. How will the change process be managed?
<--- Score

36. How difficult is it to qualify what technology evaluation ROI is?
<--- Score

37. Have any additional benefits been identified that will result from closing all or most of the gaps?
<--- Score

38. What is the oversight process?
<--- Score

39. What did the team gain from developing a sub-process map?
<--- Score

40. How do you define collaboration and team output?
<--- Score

41. Has data output been validated?
<--- Score

42. What other organizational variables, such as reward systems or communication systems, affect the performance of this technology evaluation process?
<--- Score

43. How is the way you as the leader think and process information affecting your organizational culture?
<--- Score

44. What kind of crime could a potential new hire have committed that would not only not disqualify him/her from being hired by your organization, but would actually indicate that he/she might be a particularly good fit?
<--- Score

45. Did any value-added analysis or 'lean thinking' take place to identify some of the gaps shown on the 'as is' process map?
<--- Score

46. Who is involved in the management review process?
<--- Score

47. Did any additional data need to be collected?
<--- Score

48. Should you invest in industry-recognized qualifications?
<--- Score

49. What are the disruptive technology evaluation technologies that enable your organization to radically change your business processes?
<--- Score

50. Think about some of the processes you undertake within your organization, which do you own?
<--- Score

51. How do mission and objectives affect the technology evaluation processes of your organization?
<--- Score

52. How has the technology evaluation data been gathered?
<--- Score

53. Is the final output clearly identified?
<--- Score

54. Were any designed experiments used to generate additional insight into the data analysis?
<--- Score

55. Which technology evaluation data should be retained?
<--- Score

56. What qualifies as competition?
<--- Score

57. What were the financial benefits resulting from any 'ground fruit or low-hanging fruit' (quick fixes)?
<--- Score

58. How do you identify specific technology evaluation investment opportunities and emerging trends?
<--- Score

59. Who gets your output?
<--- Score

60. When should a process be art not science?
<--- Score

61. What technology evaluation metrics are outputs of the process?
<--- Score

62. Where can you get qualified talent today?
<--- Score

63. Do your employees have the opportunity to do what they do best everyday?
<--- Score

64. Do quality systems drive continuous improvement?
<--- Score

65. How is technology evaluation data gathered?
<--- Score

66. What are your outputs?
<--- Score

67. What is the Value Stream Mapping?
<--- Score

68. A compounding model resolution with available relevant data can often provide insight towards a solution methodology; which technology evaluation models, tools and techniques are necessary?
<--- Score

69. What are your key performance measures or indicators and in-process measures for the control and improvement of your technology evaluation processes?
<--- Score

70. How can risk management be tied procedurally to process elements?
<--- Score

71. What technology evaluation data will be collected?
<--- Score

72. What are the processes for audit reporting and management?
<--- Score

73. How much data can be collected in the given timeframe?
<--- Score

74. Were Pareto charts (or similar) used to portray the

'heavy hitters' (or key sources of variation)?
<--- Score

75. Do your leaders quickly bounce back from setbacks?
<--- Score

76. What conclusions were drawn from the team's data collection and analysis? How did the team reach these conclusions?
<--- Score

77. Who will gather what data?
<--- Score

78. Have you defined which data is gathered how?
<--- Score

79. How is the technology evaluation Value Stream Mapping managed?
<--- Score

80. What tools were used to narrow the list of possible causes?
<--- Score

81. Are gaps between current performance and the goal performance identified?
<--- Score

82. What resources go in to get the desired output?
<--- Score

83. What is your organizations process which leads to recognition of value generation?
<--- Score

84. What are your best practices for minimizing technology evaluation project risk, while demonstrating incremental value and quick wins throughout the technology evaluation project lifecycle?
<--- Score

85. What qualifications and skills do you need?
<--- Score

86. What technology evaluation data should be managed?
<--- Score

87. What information qualified as important?
<--- Score

88. Are your outputs consistent?
<--- Score

89. What are evaluation criteria for the output?
<--- Score

90. Think about the functions involved in your technology evaluation project, what processes flow from these functions?
<--- Score

91. What are the personnel training and qualifications required?
<--- Score

92. Is pre-qualification of suppliers carried out?
<--- Score

93. Identify an operational issue in your organization, for example, could a particular task be done more quickly or more efficiently by technology evaluation?
<--- Score

94. What are the technology evaluation business drivers?
<--- Score

95. Is the gap/opportunity displayed and communicated in financial terms?
<--- Score

96. How was the detailed process map generated, verified, and validated?
<--- Score

97. Can you add value to the current technology evaluation decision-making process (largely qualitative) by incorporating uncertainty modeling (more quantitative)?
<--- Score

98. Are you missing technology evaluation opportunities?
<--- Score

99. How many input/output points does it require?
<--- Score

100. Do you understand your management processes today?
<--- Score

101. What tools were used to generate the list of possible causes?

<--- Score

102. What are the necessary qualifications?
<--- Score

103. What other jobs or tasks affect the performance of the steps in the technology evaluation process?
<--- Score

104. What technology evaluation data should be collected?
<--- Score

105. What process improvements will be needed?
<--- Score

106. What qualifications are needed?
<--- Score

107. What technology evaluation data do you gather or use now?
<--- Score

108. What methods do you use to gather technology evaluation data?
<--- Score

109. Do you, as a leader, bounce back quickly from setbacks?
<--- Score

110. Who will facilitate the team and process?
<--- Score

111. What data is gathered?
<--- Score

112. Has an output goal been set?
<--- Score

113. How do you use technology evaluation data and information to support organizational decision making and innovation?
<--- Score

114. Were there any improvement opportunities identified from the process analysis?
<--- Score

115. What quality tools were used to get through the analyze phase?
<--- Score

116. Where is the data coming from to measure compliance?
<--- Score

117. Where is technology evaluation data gathered?
<--- Score

118. Who owns what data?
<--- Score

119. Is there an established change management process?
<--- Score

120. Is the required technology evaluation data gathered?
<--- Score

121. Who is involved with workflow mapping?

<--- Score

122. An organizationally feasible system request is one that considers the mission, goals and objectives of the organization, key questions are: is the technology evaluation solution request practical and will it solve a problem or take advantage of an opportunity to achieve company goals?
<--- Score

123. Are technology evaluation changes recognized early enough to be approved through the regular process?
<--- Score

124. What data do you need to collect?
<--- Score

125. What, related to, technology evaluation processes does your organization outsource?
<--- Score

126. What are the best opportunities for value improvement?
<--- Score

127. What will drive technology evaluation change?
<--- Score

128. How will the data be checked for quality?
<--- Score

129. Is there a strict change management process?
<--- Score

130. What are the revised rough estimates of the

financial savings/opportunity for technology evaluation improvements?

<--- Score

131. Do you have the authority to produce the output?

<--- Score

132. How is the data gathered?

<--- Score

133. What are your current levels and trends in key technology evaluation measures or indicators of product and process performance that are important to and directly serve your customers?

<--- Score

Add up total points for this section:

_ _ _ _ _ = Total points for this section

Divided by: _ _ _ _ _ _ (number of statements answered) = _ _ _ _ _ _ Average score for this section

Transfer your score to the technology evaluation Index at the beginning of the Self-Assessment.

CRITERION #5: IMPROVE:

INTENT: Develop a practical solution. Innovate, establish and test the solution and to measure the results.

In my belief, the answer to this question is clearly defined:

5 Strongly Agree

4 Agree

3 Neutral

2 Disagree

1 Strongly Disagree

1. How risky is your organization?
<--- Score

2. What are your current levels and trends in key measures or indicators of workforce and leader development?
<--- Score

3. **Have you achieved technology evaluation**

improvements?

<--- Score

4. Is there any other technology evaluation solution?

<--- Score

5. Who makes the technology evaluation decisions in your organization?

<--- Score

6. Who controls key decisions that will be made?

<--- Score

7. Who will be responsible for documenting the technology evaluation requirements in detail?

<--- Score

8. What is the team's contingency plan for potential problems occurring in implementation?

<--- Score

9. Were any criteria developed to assist the team in testing and evaluating potential solutions?

<--- Score

10. What criteria will you use to assess your technology evaluation risks?

<--- Score

11. Who are the key stakeholders for the technology evaluation evaluation?

<--- Score

12. Do those selected for the technology evaluation team have a good general understanding of what technology evaluation is

all about?
<--- Score

13. What were the underlying assumptions on the cost-benefit analysis?
<--- Score

14. How do you manage and improve your technology evaluation work systems to deliver customer value and achieve organizational success and sustainability?
<--- Score

15. Is the technology evaluation risk managed?
<--- Score

16. Is any technology evaluation documentation required?
<--- Score

17. What is the implementation plan?
<--- Score

18. Do vendor agreements bring new compliance risk ?
<--- Score

19. Are the most efficient solutions problem-specific?
<--- Score

20. Who are the technology evaluation decision makers?
<--- Score

21. What went well, what should change, what can improve?

<--- Score

22. Risk Identification: What are the possible risk events your organization faces in relation to technology evaluation?
<--- Score

23. What communications are necessary to support the implementation of the solution?
<--- Score

24. What is technology evaluation's impact on utilizing the best solution(s)?
<--- Score

25. Are the risks fully understood, reasonable and manageable?
<--- Score

26. What is the technology evaluation's sustainability risk?
<--- Score

27. What to do with the results or outcomes of measurements?
<--- Score

28. What are the implications of the one critical technology evaluation decision 10 minutes, 10 months, and 10 years from now?
<--- Score

29. At what point will vulnerability assessments be performed once technology evaluation is put into production (e.g., ongoing Risk Management after implementation)?

<--- Score

30. Are the key business and technology risks being managed?
<--- Score

31. What attendant changes will need to be made to ensure that the solution is successful?
<--- Score

32. How will you recognize and celebrate results?
<--- Score

33. How does the team improve its work?
<--- Score

34. Is the measure of success for technology evaluation understandable to a variety of people?
<--- Score

35. Does a good decision guarantee a good outcome?
<--- Score

36. What are the affordable technology evaluation risks?
<--- Score

37. What is the magnitude of the improvements?
<--- Score

38. Are decisions made in a timely manner?
<--- Score

39. Who should make the technology evaluation decisions?

<--- Score

40. Where do you need technology evaluation improvement?
<--- Score

41. What strategies for technology evaluation improvement are successful?
<--- Score

42. How will you measure the results?
<--- Score

43. What do you want to improve?
<--- Score

44. Risk events: what are the things that could go wrong?
<--- Score

45. Is there a high likelihood that any recommendations will achieve their intended results?
<--- Score

46. Is the solution technically practical?
<--- Score

47. What is technology evaluation risk?
<--- Score

48. What actually has to improve and by how much?
<--- Score

49. How risky is your organization?
<--- Score

50. How can you improve performance?
<--- Score

51. What tools were used to tap into the creativity and encourage 'outside the box' thinking?
<--- Score

52. How can skill-level changes improve technology evaluation?
<--- Score

53. How do you measure risk?
<--- Score

54. What does the 'should be' process map/design look like?
<--- Score

55. What tools were most useful during the improve phase?
<--- Score

56. What tools do you use once you have decided on a technology evaluation strategy and more importantly how do you choose?
<--- Score

57. Who manages technology evaluation risk?
<--- Score

58. How do you decide how much to remunerate an employee?
<--- Score

59. How do you manage technology evaluation risk?
<--- Score

60. Are procedures documented for managing technology evaluation risks?

<--- Score

61. Do you combine technical expertise with business knowledge and technology evaluation Key topics include lifecycles, development approaches, requirements and how to make a business case?

<--- Score

62. Was a technology evaluation charter developed?

<--- Score

63. How do you go about comparing technology evaluation approaches/solutions?

<--- Score

64. What tools were used to evaluate the potential solutions?

<--- Score

65. How is knowledge sharing about risk management improved?

<--- Score

66. Will the controls trigger any other risks?

<--- Score

67. What lessons, if any, from a pilot were incorporated into the design of the full-scale solution?

<--- Score

68. What are the technology evaluation security risks?

<--- Score

69. How do you improve technology evaluation service perception, and satisfaction?
<--- Score

70. How does your organization evaluate strategic technology evaluation success?

<--- Score

71. How do you deal with technology evaluation risk?

<--- Score

72. Do you have the optimal project management team structure?
<--- Score

73. How are technology evaluation risks managed?
<--- Score

74. How do you define the solutions' scope?
<--- Score

75. What should a proof of concept or pilot accomplish?

<--- Score

76. Who do you report technology evaluation results to?

<--- Score

77. How is continuous improvement applied to risk management?
<--- Score

78. Risk factors: what are the characteristics of technology evaluation that make it risky?

<--- Score

79. How will you know that a change is an improvement?
<--- Score

80. If you could go back in time five years, what decision would you make differently? What is your best guess as to what decision you're making today you might regret five years from now?
<--- Score

81. What practices helps your organization to develop its capacity to recognize patterns?
<--- Score

82. How are policy decisions made and where?
<--- Score

83. How do you link measurement and risk?
<--- Score

84. Is the technology evaluation documentation thorough?
<--- Score

85. To what extent does management recognize technology evaluation as a tool to increase the results?
<--- Score

86. Is risk periodically assessed?
<--- Score

87. Is supporting technology evaluation documentation required?

<--- Score

88. How do you improve productivity?
<--- Score

89. Have you identified breakpoints and/or risk tolerances that will trigger broad consideration of a potential need for intervention or modification of strategy?
<--- Score

90. Would you develop a technology evaluation Communication Strategy?
<--- Score

91. How do the technology evaluation results compare with the performance of your competitors and other organizations with similar offerings?
<--- Score

92. What risks do you need to manage?
<--- Score

93. When you map the key players in your own work and the types/domains of relationships with them, which relationships do you find easy and which challenging, and why?
<--- Score

94. What are the expected technology evaluation results?
<--- Score

95. Explorations of the frontiers of technology evaluation will help you build influence, improve

technology evaluation, optimize decision making, and sustain change, what is your approach?

<--- Score

96. How do you keep improving technology evaluation?

<--- Score

97. Who manages supplier risk management in your organization?

<--- Score

98. What resources are required for the improvement efforts?

<--- Score

99. How can the phases of technology evaluation development be identified?

<--- Score

100. How significant is the improvement in the eyes of the end user?

<--- Score

101. What improvements have been achieved?

<--- Score

102. Is the scope clearly documented?

<--- Score

103. How do you mitigate technology evaluation risk?

<--- Score

104. What are the concrete technology evaluation results?

<--- Score

105. Are events managed to resolution?
<--- Score

106. How will you know that you have improved?
<--- Score

107. Do you need to do a usability evaluation?
<--- Score

108. What were the criteria for evaluating a technology evaluation pilot?
<--- Score

109. Are risk triggers captured?
<--- Score

110. Which of the recognised risks out of all risks can be most likely transferred?
<--- Score

111. In the past few months, what is the smallest change you have made that has had the biggest positive result? What was it about that small change that produced the large return?
<--- Score

112. Are you assessing technology evaluation and risk?
<--- Score

113. What error proofing will be done to address some of the discrepancies observed in the 'as is' process?
<--- Score

114. Does the goal represent a desired result that can

be measured?
<--- Score

115. What technology evaluation improvements can be made?
<--- Score

116. How scalable is your technology evaluation solution?
<--- Score

117. Can you identify any significant risks or exposures to technology evaluation third- parties (vendors, service providers, alliance partners etc) that concern you?
<--- Score

118. Who will be using the results of the measurement activities?
<--- Score

119. Who controls the risk?
<--- Score

120. What is the risk?
<--- Score

121. For decision problems, how do you develop a decision statement?
<--- Score

122. Do you cover the five essential competencies: Communication, Collaboration,Innovation, Adaptability, and Leadership that improve an organizations ability to leverage the new technology evaluation in a volatile global economy?

<--- Score

123. What needs improvement? Why?
<--- Score

124. Why improve in the first place?
<--- Score

125. Can you integrate quality management and risk management?
<--- Score

126. How can you improve technology evaluation?
<--- Score

127. How do you improve your likelihood of success ?
<--- Score

128. Where do the technology evaluation decisions reside?
<--- Score

129. How do you measure improved technology evaluation service perception, and satisfaction?
<--- Score

130. Which technology evaluation solution is appropriate?
<--- Score

131. How will you know when its improved?
<--- Score

Add up total points for this section:
_ _ _ _ _ = Total points for this section

Divided by: _____ (number of
statements answered) = _____
Average score for this section

Transfer your score to the technology
evaluation Index at the beginning of
the Self-Assessment.

CRITERION #6: CONTROL:

INTENT: Implement the practical solution. Maintain the performance and correct possible complications.

In my belief, the answer to this question is clearly defined:

5 Strongly Agree

4 Agree

3 Neutral

2 Disagree

1 Strongly Disagree

1. Where do ideas that reach policy makers and planners as proposals for technology evaluation strengthening and reform actually originate?
<--- Score

2. What key inputs and outputs are being measured on an ongoing basis?
<--- Score

3. What other areas of the group might benefit from the technology evaluation team's improvements, knowledge, and learning?
<--- Score

4. What do you measure to verify effectiveness gains?
<--- Score

5. Is there a technology evaluation Communication plan covering who needs to get what information when?
<--- Score

6. Can support from partners be adjusted?
<--- Score

7. How do your controls stack up?
<--- Score

8. How will report readings be checked to effectively monitor performance?
<--- Score

9. How do you plan on providing proper recognition and disclosure of supporting companies?
<--- Score

10. What do you stand for--and what are you against?
<--- Score

11. How is change control managed?
<--- Score

12. Has the technology evaluation value of standards been quantified?
<--- Score

13. Are there documented procedures?
<--- Score

14. How do controls support value?
<--- Score

15. Is the technology evaluation test/monitoring cost justified?
<--- Score

16. Does the response plan contain a definite closed loop continual improvement scheme (e.g., plan-do-check-act)?
<--- Score

17. Can you adapt and adjust to changing technology evaluation situations?
<--- Score

18. Is there a recommended audit plan for routine surveillance inspections of technology evaluation's gains?
<--- Score

19. How will input, process, and output variables be checked to detect for sub-optimal conditions?
<--- Score

20. You may have created your quality measures at a time when you lacked resources, technology wasn't up to the required standard, or low service levels were the industry norm. Have those circumstances changed?
<--- Score

21. What should the next improvement project be that is related to technology evaluation?
<--- Score

22. Will the team be available to assist members in planning investigations?
<--- Score

23. How do you encourage people to take control and responsibility?
<--- Score

24. Is there a control plan in place for sustaining improvements (short and long-term)?
<--- Score

25. Are the technology evaluation standards challenging?
<--- Score

26. Is there documentation that will support the successful operation of the improvement?
<--- Score

27. What is the control/monitoring plan?
<--- Score

28. Is reporting being used or needed?
<--- Score

29. Do the technology evaluation decisions you make today help people and the planet tomorrow?
<--- Score

30. Does technology evaluation appropriately measure and monitor risk?

<--- Score

31. Is a response plan established and deployed?
<--- Score

32. Are pertinent alerts monitored, analyzed and distributed to appropriate personnel?
<--- Score

33. How widespread is its use?
<--- Score

34. Are suggested corrective/restorative actions indicated on the response plan for known causes to problems that might surface?
<--- Score

35. Will any special training be provided for results interpretation?
<--- Score

36. Are operating procedures consistent?
<--- Score

37. What are your results for key measures or indicators of the accomplishment of your technology evaluation strategy and action plans, including building and strengthening core competencies?
<--- Score

38. In the case of a technology evaluation project, the criteria for the audit derive from implementation objectives, an audit of a technology evaluation project involves assessing whether the recommendations outlined for implementation have been met, can

you track that any technology evaluation project is implemented as planned, and is it working?
<--- Score

39. How do you plan for the cost of succession?
<--- Score

40. What quality tools were useful in the control phase?
<--- Score

41. Against what alternative is success being measured?
<--- Score

42. How do you select, collect, align, and integrate technology evaluation data and information for tracking daily operations and overall organizational performance, including progress relative to strategic objectives and action plans?
<--- Score

43. How will the process owner verify improvement in present and future sigma levels, process capabilities?
<--- Score

44. What is the standard for acceptable technology evaluation performance?
<--- Score

45. Is there an action plan in case of emergencies?
<--- Score

46. Is there a documented and implemented monitoring plan?
<--- Score

47. Who sets the technology evaluation standards?
<--- Score

48. What is the recommended frequency of auditing?
<--- Score

49. Does job training on the documented procedures need to be part of the process team's education and training?
<--- Score

50. What do your reports reflect?
<--- Score

51. Will your goals reflect your program budget?
<--- Score

52. How will technology evaluation decisions be made and monitored?
<--- Score

53. Is knowledge gained on process shared and institutionalized?
<--- Score

54. Do you monitor the effectiveness of your technology evaluation activities?
<--- Score

55. Implementation Planning: is a pilot needed to test the changes before a full roll out occurs?
<--- Score

56. Is new knowledge gained imbedded in the response plan?

<--- Score

57. How do senior leaders actions reflect a commitment to the organizations technology evaluation values?
<--- Score

58. Is there a standardized process?
<--- Score

59. How do you monitor usage and cost?
<--- Score

60. Will existing staff require re-training, for example, to learn new business processes?
<--- Score

61. How do you spread information?
<--- Score

62. How will new or emerging customer needs/requirements be checked/communicated to orient the process toward meeting the new specifications and continually reducing variation?
<--- Score

63. What are you attempting to measure/monitor?
<--- Score

64. How will the process owner and team be able to hold the gains?
<--- Score

65. How will you measure your QA plan's effectiveness?
<--- Score

66. What should you measure to verify efficiency gains?

<--- Score

67. What can you control?

<--- Score

68. What are the known security controls?

<--- Score

69. Has the improved process and its steps been standardized?

<--- Score

70. How likely is the current technology evaluation plan to come in on schedule or on budget?

<--- Score

71. What are customers monitoring?

<--- Score

72. Are documented procedures clear and easy to follow for the operators?

<--- Score

73. Who controls critical resources?

<--- Score

74. Act/Adjust: What Do you Need to Do Differently?

<--- Score

75. Do you monitor the technology evaluation decisions made and fine tune them as they evolve?

<--- Score

76. What are the performance and scale of the technology evaluation tools?
<--- Score

77. How can you best use all of your knowledge repositories to enhance learning and sharing?
<--- Score

78. Are the planned controls in place?
<--- Score

79. What is the best design framework for technology evaluation organization now that, in a post industrial-age if the top-down, command and control model is no longer relevant?
<--- Score

80. Is there a transfer of ownership and knowledge to process owner and process team tasked with the responsibilities.
<--- Score

81. Does a troubleshooting guide exist or is it needed?
<--- Score

82. Have new or revised work instructions resulted?
<--- Score

83. How will the day-to-day responsibilities for monitoring and continual improvement be transferred from the improvement team to the process owner?
<--- Score

84. Are new process steps, standards, and

documentation ingrained into normal operations?
<--- Score

85. Who is the technology evaluation process owner?
<--- Score

86. Are the planned controls working?
<--- Score

87. What are the key elements of your technology evaluation performance improvement system, including your evaluation, organizational learning, and innovation processes?
<--- Score

88. What technology evaluation standards are applicable?
<--- Score

89. What are the critical parameters to watch?
<--- Score

90. Do the viable solutions scale to future needs?
<--- Score

91. Are controls in place and consistently applied?
<--- Score

92. Does the technology evaluation performance meet the customer's requirements?
<--- Score

93. How might the group capture best practices and lessons learned so as to leverage improvements?
<--- Score

94. How do you establish and deploy modified action plans if circumstances require a shift in plans and rapid execution of new plans?
<--- Score

95. What other systems, operations, processes, and infrastructures (hiring practices, staffing, training, incentives/rewards, metrics/dashboards/scorecards, etc.) need updates, additions, changes, or deletions in order to facilitate knowledge transfer and improvements?
<--- Score

96. Are you measuring, monitoring and predicting technology evaluation activities to optimize operations and profitability, and enhancing outcomes?
<--- Score

97. What adjustments to the strategies are needed?
<--- Score

98. Who is going to spread your message?
<--- Score

99. Is a response plan in place for when the input, process, or output measures indicate an 'out-of-control' condition?
<--- Score

Add up total points for this section:
_ _ _ _ _ = Total points for this section

Divided by: _ _ _ _ _ _ (number of statements answered) = _ _ _ _ _ _

Average score for this section

Transfer your score to the technology
evaluation Index at the beginning of
the Self-Assessment.

CRITERION #7: SUSTAIN:

INTENT: Retain the benefits.

In my belief, the answer to this question is clearly defined:

5 Strongly Agree

4 Agree

3 Neutral

2 Disagree

1 Strongly Disagree

1. What are your most important goals for the strategic technology evaluation objectives?
<--- Score

2. Who is responsible for ensuring appropriate resources (time, people and money) are allocated to technology evaluation?
<--- Score

3. What are you challenging?
<--- Score

4. Is your strategy driving your strategy? Or is the way in which you allocate resources driving your strategy?
<--- Score

5. How much contingency will be available in the budget?
<--- Score

6. What should you stop doing?
<--- Score

7. How do you manage technology evaluation Knowledge Management (KM)?
<--- Score

8. How do you ensure that implementations of technology evaluation products are done in a way that ensures safety?
<--- Score

9. Can you do all this work?
<--- Score

10. How likely is it that a customer would recommend your company to a friend or colleague?
<--- Score

11. How do you stay inspired?
<--- Score

12. What trouble can you get into?
<--- Score

13. Will there be any necessary staff changes

(redundancies or new hires)?
<--- Score

14. Who are four people whose careers you have enhanced?
<--- Score

15. Why is it important to have senior management support for a technology evaluation project?
<--- Score

16. Do you see more potential in people than they do in themselves?
<--- Score

17. At what moment would you think; Will I get fired?
<--- Score

18. How do you determine the key elements that affect technology evaluation workforce satisfaction, how are these elements determined for different workforce groups and segments?
<--- Score

19. Who uses your product in ways you never expected?
<--- Score

20. What technology evaluation skills are most important?
<--- Score

21. What are your personal philosophies regarding technology evaluation and how do they influence your work?
<--- Score

22. Whom among your colleagues do you trust, and for what?
<--- Score

23. What is your competitive advantage?
<--- Score

24. Who is responsible for errors?
<--- Score

25. What are the success criteria that will indicate that technology evaluation objectives have been met and the benefits delivered?
<--- Score

26. Are you changing as fast as the world around you?
<--- Score

27. What new services of functionality will be implemented next with technology evaluation ?
<--- Score

28. What trophy do you want on your mantle?
<--- Score

29. How do you listen to customers to obtain actionable information?
<--- Score

30. Who is on the team?
<--- Score

31. How can you incorporate support to ensure safe and effective use of technology evaluation into the services that you provide?

<--- Score

32. Are you relevant? Will you be relevant five years from now? Ten?
<--- Score

33. How do you provide a safe environment -physically and emotionally?
<--- Score

34. How do you know if you are successful?
<--- Score

35. Can you break it down?
<--- Score

36. What are internal and external technology evaluation relations?
<--- Score

37. What are the long-term technology evaluation goals?
<--- Score

38. Who do you want your customers to become?
<--- Score

39. Have new benefits been realized?
<--- Score

40. How do you keep the momentum going?
<--- Score

41. Do you know what you are doing? And who do you call if you don't?
<--- Score

42. How do you accomplish your long range technology evaluation goals?
<--- Score

43. Who are the key stakeholders?
<--- Score

44. What is the overall talent health of your organization as a whole at senior levels, and for each organization reporting to a member of the Senior Leadership Team?
<--- Score

45. Can you maintain your growth without detracting from the factors that have contributed to your success?
<--- Score

46. Who are your customers?
<--- Score

47. How do you create buy-in?
<--- Score

48. How can you negotiate technology evaluation successfully with a stubborn boss, an irate client, or a deceitful coworker?
<--- Score

49. How much does technology evaluation help?
<--- Score

50. What projects are going on in the organization today, and what resources are those projects using from the resource pools?

<--- Score

51. What are current technology evaluation paradigms?
<--- Score

52. What is the source of the strategies for technology evaluation strengthening and reform?
<--- Score

53. What are the usability implications of technology evaluation actions?
<--- Score

54. Do you have past technology evaluation successes?
<--- Score

55. Are your responses positive or negative?
<--- Score

56. What is your BATNA (best alternative to a negotiated agreement)?
<--- Score

57. Is maximizing technology evaluation protection the same as minimizing technology evaluation loss?
<--- Score

58. What did you miss in the interview for the worst hire you ever made?
<--- Score

59. Who will provide the final approval of technology evaluation deliverables?
<--- Score

60. Do you have the right capabilities and capacities?
<--- Score

61. What must you excel at?
<--- Score

62. What management system can you use to leverage the technology evaluation experience, ideas, and concerns of the people closest to the work to be done?
<--- Score

63. What are the essentials of internal technology evaluation management?
<--- Score

64. Are you satisfied with your current role? If not, what is missing from it?
<--- Score

65. What are the challenges?
<--- Score

66. Are you / should you be revolutionary or evolutionary?
<--- Score

67. What have been your experiences in defining long range technology evaluation goals?
<--- Score

68. What are the gaps in your knowledge and experience?
<--- Score

69. Who is the main stakeholder, with ultimate responsibility for driving technology evaluation forward?
<--- Score

70. What will be the consequences to the stakeholder (financial, reputation etc) if technology evaluation does not go ahead or fails to deliver the objectives?
<--- Score

71. Is technology evaluation realistic, or are you setting yourself up for failure?
<--- Score

72. Who will manage the integration of tools?
<--- Score

73. How do you track customer value, profitability or financial return, organizational success, and sustainability?
<--- Score

74. What does your signature ensure?
<--- Score

75. In retrospect, of the projects that you pulled the plug on, what percent do you wish had been allowed to keep going, and what percent do you wish had ended earlier?
<--- Score

76. What are the short and long-term technology evaluation goals?
<--- Score

77. Think of your technology evaluation project, what are the main functions?
<--- Score

78. Do technology evaluation rules make a reasonable demand on a users capabilities?
<--- Score

79. How is implementation research currently incorporated into each of your goals?
<--- Score

80. Are the assumptions believable and achievable?
<--- Score

81. Is your basic point _____ or _____?
<--- Score

82. Were lessons learned captured and communicated?
<--- Score

83. What is the estimated value of the project?
<--- Score

84. How are you doing compared to your industry?
<--- Score

85. How will you know that the technology evaluation project has been successful?
<--- Score

86. Do you have the right people on the bus?
<--- Score

87. What is the kind of project structure that would

be appropriate for your technology evaluation project, should it be formal and complex, or can it be less formal and relatively simple?

<--- Score

88. Where can you break convention?
<--- Score

89. Is the technology evaluation organization completing tasks effectively and efficiently?
<--- Score

90. Which functions and people interact with the supplier and or customer?

<--- Score

91. If you find that you havent accomplished one of the goals for one of the steps of the technology evaluation strategy, what will you do to fix it?

<--- Score

92. What are the key enablers to make this technology evaluation move?
<--- Score

93. What relationships among technology evaluation trends do you perceive?

<--- Score

94. Is there any existing technology evaluation governance structure?
<--- Score

95. What are the barriers to increased technology evaluation production?

<--- Score

96. Who is responsible for technology evaluation?
<--- Score

97. What role does communication play in the success or failure of a technology evaluation project?
<--- Score

98. How do you assess the technology evaluation pitfalls that are inherent in implementing it?
<--- Score

99. How do you maintain technology evaluation's Integrity?
<--- Score

100. Who have you, as a company, historically been when you've been at your best?
<--- Score

101. Who do you think the world wants your organization to be?
<--- Score

102. Political -is anyone trying to undermine this project?
<--- Score

103. If you were responsible for initiating and implementing major changes in your organization, what steps might you take to ensure acceptance of those changes?
<--- Score

104. What you are going to do to affect the numbers?
<--- Score

105. Are you maintaining a past–present–future perspective throughout the technology evaluation discussion?

<--- Score

106. What one word do you want to own in the minds of your customers, employees, and partners?

<--- Score

107. Who will be responsible for deciding whether technology evaluation goes ahead or not after the initial investigations?

<--- Score

108. Do you say no to customers for no reason?

<--- Score

109. What are you trying to prove to yourself, and how might it be hijacking your life and business success?

<--- Score

110. How do you foster innovation?

<--- Score

111. What is the big technology evaluation idea?

<--- Score

112. What is the craziest thing you can do?

<--- Score

113. Who else should you help?

<--- Score

114. If no one would ever find out about your accomplishments, how would you lead differently?

<--- Score

115. What is a feasible sequencing of reform initiatives over time?
<--- Score

116. What happens when a new employee joins the organization?
<--- Score

117. What was the last experiment you ran?
<--- Score

118. How do you lead with technology evaluation in mind?
<--- Score

119. Marketing budgets are tighter, consumers are more skeptical, and social media has changed forever the way we talk about technology evaluation, how do you gain traction?
<--- Score

120. How can you become more high-tech but still be high touch?
<--- Score

121. How do senior leaders deploy your organizations vision and values through your leadership system, to the workforce, to key suppliers and partners, and to customers and other stakeholders, as appropriate?
<--- Score

122. What could happen if you do not do it?
<--- Score

123. What counts that you are not counting?

<--- Score

124. What are strategies for increasing support and reducing opposition?

<--- Score

125. Why do and why don't your customers like your organization?

<--- Score

126. What potential megatrends could make your business model obsolete?

<--- Score

127. Why is technology evaluation important for you now?

<--- Score

128. What is effective technology evaluation?

<--- Score

129. Is the impact that technology evaluation has shown?

<--- Score

130. What do we do when new problems arise?

<--- Score

131. If your customer were your grandmother, would you tell her to buy what you're selling?

<--- Score

132. Whose voice (department, ethnic group, women, older workers, etc) might you have missed hearing from in your company, and how might you amplify

this voice to create positive momentum for your business?

<--- Score

133. What is your question? Why?

<--- Score

134. How important is technology evaluation to the user organizations mission?

<--- Score

135. If you had to leave your organization for a year and the only communication you could have with employees/colleagues was a single paragraph, what would you write?

<--- Score

136. What knowledge, skills and characteristics mark a good technology evaluation project manager?

<--- Score

137. Would you rather sell to knowledgeable and informed customers or to uninformed customers?

<--- Score

138. Do you know who is a friend or a foe?

<--- Score

139. Are you paying enough attention to the partners your company depends on to succeed?

<--- Score

140. Do you have enough freaky customers in your portfolio pushing you to the limit day in and day out?

<--- Score

141. Are you making progress, and are you making progress as technology evaluation leaders?
<--- Score

142. What is it like to work for you?
<--- Score

143. Is there any reason to believe the opposite of my current belief?
<--- Score

144. How do customers see your organization?
<--- Score

145. How do you go about securing technology evaluation?
<--- Score

146. Ask yourself: how would you do this work if you only had one staff member to do it?
<--- Score

147. Are there any activities that you can take off your to do list?
<--- Score

148. How do you set technology evaluation stretch targets and how do you get people to not only participate in setting these stretch targets but also that they strive to achieve these?
<--- Score

149. Is it economical; do you have the time and money?
<--- Score

150. Do you think technology evaluation accomplishes the goals you expect it to accomplish?

<--- Score

151. In a project to restructure technology evaluation outcomes, which stakeholders would you involve?

<--- Score

152. Are all key stakeholders present at all Structured Walkthroughs?

<--- Score

153. Will it be accepted by users?

<--- Score

154. What are specific technology evaluation rules to follow?

<--- Score

155. What is the recommended frequency of auditing?

<--- Score

156. What are the rules and assumptions your industry operates under? What if the opposite were true?

<--- Score

157. Why not do technology evaluation?

<--- Score

158. Do you feel that more should be done in the technology evaluation area?

<--- Score

159. Have benefits been optimized with all key stakeholders?

<--- Score

160. What is your formula for success in technology evaluation ?

<--- Score

161. What are the potential basics of technology evaluation fraud?

<--- Score

162. Has implementation been effective in reaching specified objectives so far?

<--- Score

163. Which technology evaluation goals are the most important?

<--- Score

164. If you had to rebuild your organization without any traditional competitive advantages (i.e., no killer technology, promising research, innovative product/ service delivery model, etcetera), how would your people have to approach their work and collaborate together in order to create the necessary conditions for success?

<--- Score

165. How do you engage the workforce, in addition to satisfying them?

<--- Score

166. How will you motivate the stakeholders with the least vested interest?

<--- Score

167. How does technology evaluation integrate with other stakeholder initiatives?

<--- Score

168. If your company went out of business tomorrow, would anyone who doesn't get a paycheck here care?

<--- Score

169. Who do we want your customers to become?

<--- Score

170. Are the criteria for selecting recommendations stated?

<--- Score

171. What is something you believe that nearly no one agrees with you on?

<--- Score

172. What is the funding source for this project?

<--- Score

173. How will you insure seamless interoperability of technology evaluation moving forward?

<--- Score

174. What are the top 3 things at the forefront of your technology evaluation agendas for the next 3 years?

<--- Score

175. How do you foster the skills, knowledge, talents, attributes, and characteristics you want to have?

<--- Score

176. If there were zero limitations, what would you do differently?

<--- Score

177. In the past year, what have you done (or could you have done) to increase the accurate perception of your company/brand as ethical and honest?

<--- Score

178. Is a technology evaluation team work effort in place?

<--- Score

179. Are assumptions made in technology evaluation stated explicitly?

<--- Score

180. What are the business goals technology evaluation is aiming to achieve?

<--- Score

181. If you got fired and a new hire took your place, what would she do different?

<--- Score

182. How long will it take to change?

<--- Score

183. Is there a work around that you can use?

<--- Score

184. What is the purpose of technology evaluation in relation to the mission?

<--- Score

185. Are new benefits received and understood?

<--- Score

186. Are you using a design thinking approach and integrating Innovation, technology evaluation Experience, and Brand Value?
<--- Score

187. How do you deal with technology evaluation changes?
<--- Score

188. What would you recommend your friend do if he/she were facing this dilemma?
<--- Score

189. What would have to be true for the option on the table to be the best possible choice?
<--- Score

190. When information truly is ubiquitous, when reach and connectivity are completely global, when computing resources are infinite, and when a whole new set of impossibilities are not only possible, but happening, what will that do to your business?
<--- Score

191. How do you transition from the baseline to the target?
<--- Score

192. Who, on the executive team or the board, has spoken to a customer recently?
<--- Score

193. What stupid rule would you most like to kill?
<--- Score

194. To whom do you add value?
<--- Score

195. What information is critical to your organization that your executives are ignoring?
<--- Score

196. Why will customers want to buy your organizations products/services?
<--- Score

197. If you do not follow, then how to lead?
<--- Score

198. Can the schedule be done in the given time?
<--- Score

199. How do you keep records, of what?
<--- Score

200. What is the range of capabilities?
<--- Score

201. Do you have an implicit bias for capital investments over people investments?
<--- Score

202. How will you ensure you get what you expected?
<--- Score

203. Which models, tools and techniques are necessary?
<--- Score

204. What happens if you do not have enough

funding?
<--- Score

205. If you weren't already in this business, would you enter it today? And if not, what are you going to do about it?
<--- Score

206. What goals did you miss?
<--- Score

207. Which individuals, teams or departments will be involved in technology evaluation?
<--- Score

208. What unique value proposition (UVP) do you offer?
<--- Score

209. Do you think you know, or do you know you know ?
<--- Score

210. What may be the consequences for the performance of an organization if all stakeholders are not consulted regarding technology evaluation?
<--- Score

211. What business benefits will technology evaluation goals deliver if achieved?
<--- Score

212. Operational - will it work?
<--- Score

213. What is the overall business strategy?

<--- Score

Add up total points for this section:
_____ = Total points for this section

Divided by: _____ (number of
statements answered) = _____
Average score for this section

Transfer your score to the technology
evaluation Index at the beginning of
the Self-Assessment.

Technology Evaluation and Managing Projects, Criteria for Project Managers:

1.0 Initiating Process Group: Technology Evaluation

1. Have the stakeholders identified all individual requirements pertaining to business process?

2. What are the short and long term implications?

3. Professionals want to know what is expected from them what are the deliverables?

4. How will you know you did it?

5. Information sharing?

6. Does the Technology Evaluation project team have enough people to execute the Technology Evaluation project plan?

7. The Technology Evaluation project you are managing has nine stakeholders. How many channel of communications are there between corresponding stakeholders?

8. Have you evaluated the teams performance and asked for feedback?

9. First of all, should any action be taken?

10. What communication items need improvement?

11. Were decisions made in a timely manner?

12. Just how important is your work to the overall success of the Technology Evaluation project?

13. Are the changes in your Technology Evaluation project being formally requested, analyzed, and approved by the appropriate decision makers?

14. What were things that you did very well and want to do the same again on the next Technology Evaluation project?

15. How well did you do?

16. Although the Technology Evaluation project manager does not directly manage procurement and contracting activities, who does manage procurement and contracting activities in your organization then if not the PM?

17. Did you use a contractor or vendor?

18. Do you understand all business (operational), technical, resource and vendor risks associated with the Technology Evaluation project?

19. What will you do?

20. Do you know the roles & responsibilities required for this Technology Evaluation project?

1.1 Project Charter: Technology Evaluation

21. What are you striving to accomplish (measurable goal(s))?

22. What are the constraints?

23. Assumptions: what factors, for planning purposes, are you considering to be true?

24. Strategic fit: what is the strategic initiative identifier for this Technology Evaluation project?

25. Who are the stakeholders?

26. What goes into your Technology Evaluation project Charter?

27. Major high-level milestone targets: what events measure progress?

28. When do you use a Technology Evaluation project Charter?

29. How are Technology Evaluation projects different from operations?

30. Where does all this information come from?

31. How much?

32. Why is it important?

33. Who is the sponsor?

34. Why executive support?

35. What does it need to do?

36. Why the improvements?

37. How will you know a change is an improvement?

38. Who ise input and support will this Technology Evaluation project require?

39. Who manages integration?

40. Are you building in-house ?

1.2 Stakeholder Register: Technology Evaluation

41. What opportunities exist to provide communications?

42. What are the major Technology Evaluation project milestones requiring communications or providing communications opportunities?

43. Is your organization ready for change?

44. How should employers make voices heard?

45. What & Why?

46. Who is managing stakeholder engagement?

47. How much influence do they have on the Technology Evaluation project?

48. Who wants to talk about Security?

49. How will reports be created?

50. How big is the gap?

51. What is the power of the stakeholder?

1.3 Stakeholder Analysis Matrix: Technology Evaluation

52. What advantages do your organizations stakeholders have?

53. Financial reserves, likely returns?

54. Arena: in what fields are the actors active, where are they present?

55. What is the stakeholders power and status in relation to the Technology Evaluation project?

56. If the baseline is now, and if its improved it will be better than now?

57. Processes and systems, etc?

58. How does the Technology Evaluation project involve consultations or collaboration with other organizations?

59. Supporters; who are the supporters?

60. Benefit to whom?

61. What do people from other organizations see as your organizations weaknesses?

62. Participatory approach: how will key stakeholders participate in the Technology Evaluation project?

63. Inoculations or payment to receive them?

64. What is relationship with the Technology Evaluation project?

65. What is the relationship among stakeholders?

66. Economy - home, abroad?

67. Who are potential allies and opponents?

68. Are you working on the right risks?

69. Why is it important to identify them?

70. What is the stakeholders mandate, what is mission?

71. What are the reimbursement requirements?

2.0 Planning Process Group: Technology Evaluation

72. How well did the chosen processes fit the needs of the Technology Evaluation project?

73. Is your organization showing technical capacity and leadership commitment to keep working with the Technology Evaluation project and to repeat it?

74. How will users learn how to use the deliverables?

75. To what extent and in what ways are the Technology Evaluation project contributing to progress towards organizational reform?

76. Contingency planning. if a risk event occurs, what will you do?

77. To what extent have the target population and participants made the activities own, taking an active role in it?

78. How will it affect you?

79. When will the Technology Evaluation project be done?

80. In which Technology Evaluation project management process group is the detailed Technology Evaluation project budget created?

81. What makes your Technology Evaluation project

successful?

82. Explanation: is what the Technology Evaluation project intents to solve a hard question?

83. Have more efficient (sensitive) and appropriate measures been adopted to respond to the political and socio-cultural problems identified?

84. Why do it Technology Evaluation projects fail?

85. To what extent is the program helping to influence your organizations policy framework?

86. Are there efficient coordination mechanisms to avoid overloading the counterparts, participating stakeholders?

87. When developing the estimates for Technology Evaluation project phases, you choose to add the individual estimates for the activities that comprise each phase. What type of estimation method are you using?

88. Are the follow-up indicators relevant and do they meet the quality needed to measure the outputs and outcomes of the Technology Evaluation project?

89. If a task is partitionable, is this a sufficient condition to reduce the Technology Evaluation project duration?

90. How well defined and documented are the Technology Evaluation project management processes you chose to use?

2.1 Project Management Plan: Technology Evaluation

91. Has the selected plan been formulated using cost effectiveness and incremental analysis techniques?

92. Is the budget realistic?

93. Did the planning effort collaborate to develop solutions that integrate expertise, policies, programs, and Technology Evaluation projects across entities?

94. How do you manage time?

95. What if, for example, the positive direction and vision of your organization causes expected trends to change resulting in greater need than expected?

96. What does management expect of PMs?

97. Development trends and opportunities. What if the positive direction and vision of your organization causes expected trends to change?

98. What went right?

99. What happened during the process that you found interesting?

100. What are the deliverables?

101. Is the appropriate plan selected based on your organizations objectives and evaluation criteria

expressed in Principles and Guidelines policies?

102. Is the engineering content at a feasibility level-of-detail, and is it sufficiently complete, to provide an adequate basis for the baseline cost estimate?

103. What is the business need?

104. Was the peer (technical) review of the cost estimates duly coordinated with the cost estimate center of expertise and addressed in the review documentation and certification?

105. How do you manage integration?

106. Are calculations and results of analyzes essentially correct?

2.2 Scope Management Plan: Technology Evaluation

107. Are estimating assumptions and constraints captured?

108. Has the Technology Evaluation project manager been identified?

109. Is current scope of the Technology Evaluation project substantially different than that originally defined?

110. What weaknesses do you have?

111. Was the scope definition used in task sequencing?

112. Has your organization done similar tasks before?

113. Is there a requirements change management processes in place?

114. Are action items captured and managed?

115. Are schedule deliverables actually delivered?

116. Has the Technology Evaluation project approach and development strategy of the Technology Evaluation project been defined, documented and accepted by the appropriate stakeholders?

117. Has a capability assessment been conducted?

118. Is there a set of procedures defining the scope, procedures, and deliverables defining quality control?

119. Has the schedule been baselined?

120. What problem is being solved by delivering this Technology Evaluation project?

121. Organizational policies that might affect the availability of resources?

122. Were Technology Evaluation project team members involved in detailed estimating and scheduling?

123. Does the Technology Evaluation project team have the skills necessary to successfully complete current Technology Evaluation project(s) and support the application?

124. Are you doing what you have set out to do?

125. Are meeting objectives identified for each meeting?

126. Are alternatives safe, functional, constructible, economical, reasonable and sustainable?

2.3 Requirements Management Plan: Technology Evaluation

127. Have stakeholders been instructed in the Change Control process?

128. Who came up with this requirement?

129. Is there formal agreement on who has authority to request a change in requirements?

130. How do you know that you have done this right?

131. Did you get proper approvals?

132. How will unresolved questions be handled once approval has been obtained?

133. Subject to change control?

134. Has the requirements team been instructed in the Change Control process?

135. Will you use an assessment of the Technology Evaluation project environment as a tool to discover risk to the requirements process?

136. The wbs is developed as part of a joint planning session. and how do you know that youhave done this right?

137. What are you counting on?

138. How will requirements be managed?

139. When and how will a requirements baseline be established in this Technology Evaluation project?

140. How knowledgeable is the team in the proposed application area?

141. Is requirements work dependent on any other specific Technology Evaluation project or non-Technology Evaluation project activities (e.g. funding, approvals, procurement)?

142. Who will perform the analysis?

143. Is it new or replacing an existing business system or process?

144. In case of software development; Should you have a test for each code module?

145. Why manage requirements?

146. Who will initially review the Technology Evaluation project work or products to ensure it meets the applicable acceptance criteria?

2.4 Requirements Documentation: Technology Evaluation

147. Basic work/business process; high-level, what is being touched?

148. Do technical resources exist?

149. What images does it conjure?

150. What are the potential disadvantages/ advantages?

151. Can you check system requirements?

152. Has requirements gathering uncovered information that would necessitate changes?

153. How does what is being described meet the business need?

154. Who is involved?

155. What variations exist for a process?

156. Who is interacting with the system?

157. Do your constraints stand?

158. What kind of entity is a problem ?

159. How do you get the user to tell you what they want?

160. Is the origin of the requirement clearly stated?

161. What are the acceptance criteria?

162. Verifiability. can the requirements be checked?

163. What if the system wasn t implemented?

164. Where do you define what is a customer, what are the attributes of customer?

165. What are the attributes of a customer?

166. What will be the integration problems?

2.5 Requirements Traceability Matrix: Technology Evaluation

167. How small is small enough?

168. How will it affect the stakeholders personally in career?

169. What percentage of Technology Evaluation projects are producing traceability matrices between requirements and other work products?

170. Will you use a Requirements Traceability Matrix?

171. What are the chronologies, contingencies, consequences, criteria?

172. Why do you manage scope?

173. How do you manage scope?

174. Do you have a clear understanding of all subcontracts in place?

175. What is the WBS?

176. Why use a WBS?

177. Is there a requirements traceability process in place?

178. Describe the process for approving requirements so they can be added to the traceability matrix

and Technology Evaluation project work can be performed. Will the Technology Evaluation project requirements become approved in writing?

2.6 Project Scope Statement: Technology Evaluation

179. Was planning completed before the Technology Evaluation project was initiated?

180. Have you been able to easily identify success criteria and create objective measurements for each of the Technology Evaluation project scopes goal statements?

181. How often do you estimate that the scope might change, and why?

182. Are there backup strategies for key members of the Technology Evaluation project?

183. Is an issue management process documented and filed?

184. Is there a Change Management Board?

185. Will the Technology Evaluation project risks be managed according to the Technology Evaluation projects risk management process?

186. Were potential customers involved early in the planning process?

187. Will the risk status be reported to management on a regular and frequent basis?

188. Is the scope of your Technology Evaluation

project well defined?

189. If you were to write a list of what should not be included in the scope statement, what are the things that you would recommend be described as out-of-scope?

190. Are there adequate Technology Evaluation project control systems?

191. Have the configuration management functions been assigned?

192. If there is an independent oversight contractor, have they signed off on the Technology Evaluation project Plan?

193. Is there a process (test plans, inspections, reviews) defined for verifying outputs for each task?

194. How often will scope changes be reviewed?

195. Is the plan for Technology Evaluation project resources adequate?

196. Who will you recommend approve the change, and when do you recommend the change reviews occur?

197. What are the defined meeting materials?

2.7 Assumption and Constraint Log: Technology Evaluation

198. Are requirements management tracking tools and procedures in place?

199. Are there unnecessary steps that are creating bottlenecks and/or causing people to wait?

200. Is the amount of effort justified by the anticipated value of forming a new process?

201. Is there a Steering Committee in place?

202. Security analysis has access to information that is sanitized?

203. Does the system design reflect the requirements?

204. What worked well?

205. Is there adequate stakeholder participation for the vetting of requirements definition, changes and management?

206. Does the document/deliverable meet all requirements (for example, statement of work) specific to this deliverable?

207. What do you audit?

208. Is the definition of the Technology Evaluation project scope clear; what needs to be accomplished?

209. After observing execution of process, is it in compliance with the documented Plan?

210. Have all stakeholders been identified?

211. Is staff trained on the software technologies that are being used on the Technology Evaluation project?

212. Does the plan conform to standards?

213. What is positive about the current process?

214. Does a specific action and/or state that is known to violate security policy occur?

215. Are there cosmetic errors that hinder readability and comprehension?

216. Contradictory information between different documents?

2.8 Work Breakdown Structure: Technology Evaluation

217. What is the probability that the Technology Evaluation project duration will exceed xx weeks?

218. When does it have to be done?

219. Is the work breakdown structure (wbs) defined and is the scope of the Technology Evaluation project clear with assigned deliverable owners?

220. Do you need another level?

221. What has to be done?

222. Is it a change in scope?

223. What is the probability of completing the Technology Evaluation project in less that xx days?

224. Why would you develop a Work Breakdown Structure?

225. Who has to do it?

226. How much detail?

227. Is it still viable?

228. Where does it take place?

229. Why is it useful?

230. When do you stop?

231. How will you and your Technology Evaluation project team define the Technology Evaluation projects scope and work breakdown structure?

232. Can you make it?

2.9 WBS Dictionary: Technology Evaluation

233. Major functional areas of contract effort?

234. Are data elements reconcilable between internal summary reports and reports forwarded to us?

235. Software specification, development, integration, and testing, licenses ?

236. Are material costs reported within the same period as that in which BCWP is earned for that material?

237. Is subcontracted work defined and identified to the appropriate subcontractor within the proper WBS element?

238. Appropriate work authorization documents which subdivide the contractual effort and responsibilities, within functional organizations?

239. The total budget for the contract (including estimates for authorized and unpriced work)?

240. Does the scheduling system provide for the identification of work progress against technical and other milestones, and also provide for forecasts of completion dates of scheduled work?

241. Are records maintained to show how management reserves are used?

242. Contemplated overhead expenditure for each period based on the best information currently available?

243. Are detailed work packages planned as far in advance as practicable?

244. Are the bases and rates for allocating costs from each indirect pool consistently applied?

245. Detailed schedules which support control account and work package start and completion dates/events?

246. Is authorization of budgets in excess of the contract budget base controlled formally and done with the full knowledge and recognition of the procuring activity?

247. Are estimates developed by Technology Evaluation project personnel coordinated with the already stated responsible for overall management to determine whether required resources will be available according to revised planning?

248. Where learning is used in developing underlying budgets is there a direct relationship between anticipated learning and time phased budgets?

249. Are retroactive changes to budgets for completed work specifically prohibited in an established procedure, and is this procedure adhered to?

250. Are the wbs and organizational levels for

application of the Technology Evaluation projected overhead costs identified?

251. Does the contractors system identify work accomplishment against the schedule plan?

2.10 Schedule Management Plan: Technology Evaluation

252. Are the quality tools and methods identified in the Quality Plan appropriate to the Technology Evaluation project?

253. Is the schedule updated on a periodic basis?

254. What will be the final cost of the Technology Evaluation project if status quo is maintained?

255. What happens if a warning is triggered?

256. Are the key elements of a Technology Evaluation project Charter present?

257. Do Technology Evaluation project teams & team members report on status / activities / progress?

258. Are the results of quality assurance reviews provided to affected groups & individuals?

259. Which status reports are received per the Technology Evaluation project Plan?

260. Staffing Requirements?

261. Is there general agreement & acceptance of the current status and progress of the Technology Evaluation project?

262. Is it standard practice to formally commit

stakeholders to the Technology Evaluation project via agreements?

263. How relevant is this attribute to this Technology Evaluation project or audit?

264. Is the correct WBS element identified for each task and milestone in the IMS?

265. Is an industry recognized mechanized support tool(s) being used for Technology Evaluation project scheduling & tracking?

266. Cost / benefit analysis?

267. Was your organizations estimating methodology being used and followed?

268. Are vendor contract reports, reviews and visits conducted periodically?

269. Is there an excessive and invalid use of task constraints and relationships of leads/lags?

270. Are the Technology Evaluation project plans updated on a frequent basis?

2.11 Activity List: Technology Evaluation

271. What are the critical bottleneck activities?

272. For other activities, how much delay can be tolerated?

273. What will be performed?

274. How can the Technology Evaluation project be displayed graphically to better visualize the activities?

275. What is the total time required to complete the Technology Evaluation project if no delays occur?

276. How much slack is available in the Technology Evaluation project?

277. What is the LF and LS for each activity?

278. Should you include sub-activities?

279. What went wrong?

280. How will it be performed?

281. In what sequence?

282. What is the probability the Technology Evaluation project can be completed in xx weeks?

283. Are the required resources available or need to

be acquired?

284. What did not go as well?

285. How detailed should a Technology Evaluation project get?

286. When will the work be performed?

287. Is there anything planned that does not need to be here?

2.12 Activity Attributes: Technology Evaluation

288. What is missing?

289. Does your organization of the data change its meaning?

290. How difficult will it be to do specific activities on this Technology Evaluation project?

291. Is there a trend during the year?

292. Where else does it apply?

293. Have you identified the Activity Leveling Priority code value on each activity?

294. Which method produces the more accurate cost assignment?

295. Would you consider either of corresponding activities an outlier?

296. What is the general pattern here?

297. Do you feel very comfortable with your prediction?

298. How difficult will it be to complete specific activities on this Technology Evaluation project?

299. Time for overtime?

300. How much activity detail is required?

301. What activity do you think you should spend the most time on?

302. Were there other ways you could have organized the data to achieve similar results?

303. Activity: what is In the Bag?

304. Have constraints been applied to the start and finish milestones for the phases?

305. Are the required resources available?

2.13 Milestone List: Technology Evaluation

306. Calculate how long can activity be delayed?

307. Political effects?

308. Legislative effects?

309. Identify critical paths (one or more) and which activities are on the critical path?

310. Which path is the critical path?

311. How late can each activity be finished and started?

312. Do you foresee any technical risks or developmental challenges?

313. Who will manage the Technology Evaluation project on a day-to-day basis?

314. It is to be a narrative text providing the crucial aspects of your Technology Evaluation project proposal answering what, who, how, when and where?

315. Vital contracts and partners?

316. Reliability of data, plan predictability?

317. Describe the concept of the technology, product

or service that will be or has been developed. How will it be used?

318. What would happen if a delivery of material was one week late?

319. How soon can the activity start?

320. Usps (unique selling points)?

321. How difficult will it be to do specific activities on this Technology Evaluation project?

322. Obstacles faced?

323. What background experience, skills, and strengths does the team bring to your organization?

324. Effects on core activities, distraction?

325. What is the market for your technology, product or service?

2.14 Network Diagram: Technology Evaluation

326. What controls the start and finish of a job?

327. What activities must follow this activity?

328. If a current contract exists, can you provide the vendor name, contract start, and contract expiration date?

329. What are the tools?

330. What are the Major Administrative Issues?

331. Why must you schedule milestones, such as reviews, throughout the Technology Evaluation project?

332. What activity must be completed immediately before this activity can start?

333. Are the gantt chart and/or network diagram updated periodically and used to assess the overall Technology Evaluation project timetable?

334. What job or jobs could run concurrently?

335. Where do you schedule uncertainty time?

336. Where do schedules come from?

337. Exercise: what is the probability that the

Technology Evaluation project duration will exceed xx weeks?

338. Can you calculate the confidence level?

339. Planning: who, how long, what to do?

340. If the Technology Evaluation project network diagram cannot change and you have extra personnel resources, what is the BEST thing to do?

341. What job or jobs precede it?

342. What to do and When?

343. What are the Key Success Factors?

2.15 Activity Resource Requirements: Technology Evaluation

344. Which logical relationship does the PDM use most often?

345. Are there unresolved issues that need to be addressed?

346. Organizational Applicability?

347. When does monitoring begin?

348. Do you use tools like decomposition and rolling-wave planning to produce the activity list and other outputs?

349. How do you handle petty cash?

350. Why do you do that?

351. Other support in specific areas?

352. Anything else?

353. How many signatures do you require on a check and does this match what is in your policy and procedures?

354. What are constraints that you might find during the Human Resource Planning process?

355. What is the Work Plan Standard?

2.16 Resource Breakdown Structure: Technology Evaluation

356. Why is this important?

357. Who will be used as a Technology Evaluation project team member?

358. What is the difference between % Complete and % work?

359. What is Technology Evaluation project communication management?

360. Who is allowed to perform which functions?

361. What defines a successful Technology Evaluation project?

362. What can you do to improve productivity?

363. Which resources should be in the resource pool?

364. Who needs what information?

365. What is your organizations history in doing similar activities?

366. Who is allowed to see what data about which resources?

367. Who will use the system?

368. How can this help you with team building?

369. Why time management?

370. What is the primary purpose of the human resource plan?

371. What is the number one predictor of a groups productivity?

372. Any changes from stakeholders?

373. When do they need the information?

2.17 Activity Duration Estimates: Technology Evaluation

374. Consider the examples of poor quality in information technology Technology Evaluation projects presented in the What Went Wrong?

375. Do an internet search on earning pmp certification. be sure to search for yahoo groups related to this topic. what are the options you found to help people prepare for the exam?

376. How difficult will it be to do specific activities on this Technology Evaluation project?

377. Are activity duration estimates documented?

378. Does a process exist to identify individuals authorized to make certain decisions?

379. Why do you think schedule issues often cause the most conflicts on Technology Evaluation projects?

380. Is the cost performance monitored to identify variances from the plan?

381. How do theories relate to Technology Evaluation project management?

382. Do you think many other organizations could apply this methodology, or does each organization need to create its own methodology?

383. What type of information goes in a quality assurance plan?

384. What is the career outlook for Technology Evaluation project managers in information technology?

385. Are time, scope, cost, and quality monitored throughout the Technology Evaluation project?

386. Does a process exist to identify which qualified resources may be attainable?

387. Are Technology Evaluation project records organized, maintained, and assessable by Technology Evaluation project team members?

388. How do functionality, system outputs, performance, reliability, and maintainability requirements affect quality planning?

389. Do procedures exist describing how the Technology Evaluation project scope will be managed?

390. How do you enter durations, link tasks, and view critical path information?

391. Account for the four frames of organizations. How can they help Technology Evaluation project managers understand your organizational context for Technology Evaluation projects?

392. How does Technology Evaluation project management relate to other disciplines?

2.18 Duration Estimating Worksheet: Technology Evaluation

393. Define the work as completely as possible. What work will be included in the Technology Evaluation project?

394. Is this operation cost effective?

395. What questions do you have?

396. What utility impacts are there?

397. Will the Technology Evaluation project collaborate with the local community and leverage resources?

398. When do the individual activities need to start and finish?

399. Value pocket identification & quantification what are value pockets?

400. What is cost and Technology Evaluation project cost management?

401. Can the Technology Evaluation project be constructed as planned?

402. What is the total time required to complete the Technology Evaluation project if no delays occur?

403. Why estimate time and cost?

404. How should ongoing costs be monitored to try to keep the Technology Evaluation project within budget?

405. Does the Technology Evaluation project provide innovative ways for stakeholders to overcome obstacles or deliver better outcomes?

406. Do any colleagues have experience with your organization and/or RFPs?

407. Is the Technology Evaluation project responsive to community need?

408. What info is needed?

409. What is your role?

2.19 Project Schedule: Technology Evaluation

410. What documents, if any, will the subcontractor provide (eg Technology Evaluation project schedule, quality plan etc)?

411. Does the condition or event threaten the Technology Evaluation projects objectives in any ways?

412. Why do you need to manage Technology Evaluation project Risk?

413. Why do you think schedule issues often cause the most conflicts on Technology Evaluation projects?

414. How does a Technology Evaluation project get to be a year late ?

415. What does that mean?

416. Was the Technology Evaluation project schedule reviewed by all stakeholders and formally accepted?

417. Activity charts and bar charts are graphical representations of a Technology Evaluation project schedule ...how do they differ?

418. Is there a Schedule Management Plan that establishes the criteria and activities for developing, monitoring and controlling the Technology Evaluation project schedule?

419. To what degree is do you feel the entire team was committed to the Technology Evaluation project schedule?

420. Are procedures defined by which the Technology Evaluation project schedule may be changed?

421. If there are any qualifying green components to this Technology Evaluation project, what portion of the total Technology Evaluation project cost is green?

422. Why is software Technology Evaluation project disaster so common?

423. Did the Technology Evaluation project come in under budget?

424. Is infrastructure setup part of your Technology Evaluation project?

425. Your Technology Evaluation project management plan results in a Technology Evaluation project schedule that is too long. If the Technology Evaluation project network diagram cannot change and you have extra personnel resources, what is the BEST thing to do?

426. If you can not fix it, how do you do it differently?

427. How can you minimize or control changes to Technology Evaluation project schedules?

2.20 Cost Management Plan: Technology Evaluation

428. Has a structured approach been used to break work effort into manageable components (WBS)?

429. Is there an onboarding process in place?

430. Has the Technology Evaluation project manager been identified?

431. Are tasks tracked by hours?

432. Is there anything unique in this Technology Evaluation projects scope statement that will affect resources?

433. Are software metrics formally captured, analyzed and used as a basis for other Technology Evaluation project estimates?

434. Are any non-compliance issues that exist due to State practices communicated to your organization?

435. Is your organization certified as a broker of the products/supplies?

436. Are non-critical path items updated and agreed upon with the teams?

437. Will the earned value reporting interface between time and cost management?

438. Are status reports received per the Technology Evaluation project Plan?

439. Are change requests logged and managed?

440. Are the appropriate IT resources adequate to meet planned commitments?

441. Have all documents been archived in a Technology Evaluation project repository for each release?

442. Has a quality assurance plan been developed for the Technology Evaluation project?

443. Have all unresolved risks been documented?

444. How difficult will it be to do specific tasks on the Technology Evaluation project?

2.21 Activity Cost Estimates: Technology Evaluation

445. How do you change activities?

446. Were you satisfied with the work?

447. What is procurement?

448. Can you change your activities?

449. How do you fund change orders?

450. What skill level is required to do the job?

451. Based on your Technology Evaluation project communication management plan, what worked well?

452. Where can you get activity reports?

453. What were things that you did well, and could improve, and how?

454. Certification of actual expenditures?

455. Review – what are some common errors in activities to avoid?

456. Who determines when the contractor is paid?

457. What defines a successful Technology Evaluation project?

458. What happens if you cannot produce the documentation for the single audit?

459. Are cost subtotals needed?

460. How and when do you enter into Technology Evaluation project Procurement Management?

461. What is the estimators estimating history?

462. How do you allocate indirect costs to activities?

2.22 Cost Estimating Worksheet: Technology Evaluation

463. Will the Technology Evaluation project collaborate with the local community and leverage resources?

464. What can be included?

465. Who is best positioned to know and assist in identifying corresponding factors?

466. What costs are to be estimated?

467. What additional Technology Evaluation project(s) could be initiated as a result of this Technology Evaluation project?

468. Identify the timeframe necessary to monitor progress and collect data to determine how the selected measure has changed?

469. Is it feasible to establish a control group arrangement?

470. What happens to any remaining funds not used?

471. Is the Technology Evaluation project responsive to community need?

472. Can a trend be established from historical performance data on the selected measure and are the criteria for using trend analysis or forecasting

methods met?

473. How will the results be shared and to whom?

474. What is the purpose of estimating?

475. What is the estimated labor cost today based upon this information?

476. Ask: are others positioned to know, are others credible, and will others cooperate?

477. What will others want?

478. Does the Technology Evaluation project provide innovative ways for stakeholders to overcome obstacles or deliver better outcomes?

2.23 Cost Baseline: Technology Evaluation

479. Will the Technology Evaluation project fail if the change request is not executed?

480. On time?

481. Have you identified skills that are missing from your team?

482. How do you manage cost?

483. Escalation criteria met?

484. What strengths do you have?

485. Have all the product or service deliverables been accepted by the customer?

486. What is the most important thing to do next to make your Technology Evaluation project successful?

487. What is cost and Technology Evaluation project cost management?

488. Are you meeting with your team regularly?

489. Have all approved changes to the Technology Evaluation project requirement been identified and impact on the performance, cost, and schedule baselines documented?

490. What is the consequence?

491. Is the cr within Technology Evaluation project scope?

492. What deliverables come first?

493. How fast?

494. How will cost estimates be used?

495. Review your risk triggers -have your risks changed?

2.24 Quality Management Plan: Technology Evaluation

496. Checking the completeness and appropriateness of the sampling and testing. Were the right locations/ samples tested for the right parameters?

497. What is the return on investment?

498. How are records kept in the office?

499. How will you know that a change is actually an improvement?

500. How do you decide who is responsible for signing the data reports?

501. How do your action plans support the strategic objectives?

502. Is staff trained on the software technologies that are being used on the Technology Evaluation project?

503. Can the requirements be traced to the appropriate components of the solution, as well as test scripts?

504. Have all involved stakeholders and work groups committed to the Technology Evaluation project?

505. What other teams / processes would be impacted by changes to the current process, and how?

506. Is a component/condition present?

507. Are you following the quality standards?

508. Are you meeting the quality standards?

509. Have Technology Evaluation project management standards and procedures been established and documented?

510. Does the program use modeling in the permitting or decision-making processes?

511. How do you ensure that your sampling methods and procedures meet your data quality objectives?

512. What methods are used?

513. Are formal code reviews conducted?

514. How does your organization perform analyzes to assess overall organizational performance and set priorities?

2.25 Quality Metrics: Technology Evaluation

515. Is material complete (and does it meet the standards)?

516. Where is quality now?

517. How are requirements conflicts resolved?

518. Was the overall quality better or worse than previous products?

519. Subjective quality component: customer satisfaction, how do you measure it?

520. Are quality metrics defined?

521. Have alternatives been defined in the event that failure occurs?

522. Is quality culture a competitive advantage?

523. What are your organizations expectations for its quality Technology Evaluation project?

524. What metrics do you measure?

525. Was material distributed on time?

526. Is the reporting frequency appropriate?

527. What approved evidence based screening tools

can be used?

528. Which are the right metrics to use?

529. What method of measurement do you use?

530. Are there already quality metrics available that detect nonlinear embeddings and trends similar to the users perception?

531. How do you communicate results and findings to upper management?

532. How can the effectiveness of each of the activities be measured?

2.26 Process Improvement Plan: Technology Evaluation

533. Modeling current processes is great, and will you ever see a return on that investment?

534. Management commitment at all levels?

535. What personnel are the change agents for your initiative?

536. Where do you want to be?

537. Does your process ensure quality?

538. Has a process guide to collect the data been developed?

539. What lessons have you learned so far?

540. Does explicit definition of the measures exist?

541. Has the time line required to move measurement results from the points of collection to databases or users been established?

542. What is quality and how will you ensure it?

543. Purpose of goal: the motive is determined by asking, why do you want to achieve this goal?

544. To elicit goal statements, do you ask a question such as, What do you want to achieve?

545. What personnel are the coaches for your initiative?

546. The motive is determined by asking, Why do you want to achieve this goal?

547. Who should prepare the process improvement action plan?

548. Are you making progress on the improvement framework?

549. Are you making progress on the goals?

550. Why quality management?

2.27 Responsibility Assignment Matrix: Technology Evaluation

551. What happens when others get pulled for higher priority Technology Evaluation projects?

552. Which resource planning tool provides information on resource responsibility and accountability?

553. Which Technology Evaluation project management knowledge area is least mature?

554. Identify potential or actual overruns and underruns?

555. How cost benefit analysis?

556. The anticipated business volume?

557. Changes in the nature of the overhead requirements?

558. How do you manage human resources?

559. Performance to date and material commitment?

560. Who is going to do that work?

561. The already stated responsible for overhead performance control of related costs?

562. No rs: if a task has no one listed as responsible,

who is getting the job done?

563. What are the assigned resources?

564. Incurrence of actual indirect costs in excess of budgets, by element of expense?

565. Budgets assigned to control accounts?

566. Undistributed budgets, if any?

567. What materials and procurements needed?

2.28 Roles and Responsibilities: Technology Evaluation

568. Do you take the time to clearly define roles and responsibilities on Technology Evaluation project tasks?

569. Does the team have access to and ability to use data analysis tools?

570. Are your budgets supportive of a culture of quality data?

571. Are governance roles and responsibilities documented?

572. Authority: what areas/Technology Evaluation projects in your work do you have the authority to decide upon and act on the already stated decisions?

573. Influence: what areas of organizational decision making are you able to influence when you do not have authority to make the final decision?

574. Are your policies supportive of a culture of quality data?

575. Key conclusions and recommendations: Are conclusions and recommendations relevant and acceptable?

576. Accountabilities: what are the roles and responsibilities of individual team members?

577. What should you do now to prepare yourself for a promotion, increased responsibilities or a different job?

578. To decide whether to use a quality measurement, ask how will you know when it is achieved?

579. What is working well?

580. What should you highlight for improvement?

581. What areas would you highlight for changes or improvements?

582. Have you ever been a part of this team?

583. Are Technology Evaluation project team roles and responsibilities identified and documented?

584. What should you do now to ensure that you are meeting all expectations of your current position?

585. Are the quality assurance functions and related roles and responsibilities clearly defined?

586. Was the expectation clearly communicated?

2.29 Human Resource Management Plan: Technology Evaluation

587. Does the detailed work plan match the complexity of tasks with the capabilities of personnel?

588. Is it standard practice to formally commit stakeholders to the Technology Evaluation project via agreements?

589. Have Technology Evaluation project team accountabilities & responsibilities been clearly defined?

590. Are all resource assumptions documented?

591. Are Technology Evaluation project team members involved in detailed estimating and scheduling?

592. Has the scope management document been updated and distributed to help prevent scope creep?

593. Quality assurance overheads?

594. Are status reports received per the Technology Evaluation project Plan?

595. Responsiveness to change and the resulting demands for different skills and abilities?

596. Is there a formal process for updating the Technology Evaluation project baseline?

597. What areas were overlooked on this Technology Evaluation project?

598. Do people have the competencies to meet the strategic objectives?

599. Are changes in deliverable commitments agreed to by all affected groups & individuals?

600. How does the proposed individual meet each requirement?

601. Are enough systems & user personnel assigned to the Technology Evaluation project?

602. Were stakeholders aware and supportive of the principles and practices of modern cost estimation?

603. Is the quality assurance team identified?

604. Are cause and effect determined for risks when others occur?

605. Are issues raised, assessed, actioned, and resolved in a timely and efficient manner?

2.30 Communications Management Plan: Technology Evaluation

606. Which stakeholders can influence others?

607. Who is responsible?

608. Who did you turn to if you had questions?

609. Who is the stakeholder?

610. What data is going to be required?

611. Who is involved as you identify stakeholders?

612. Who to share with?

613. What is the political influence?

614. Why is stakeholder engagement important?

615. Are the stakeholders getting the information others need, are others consulted, are concerns addressed?

616. Who to learn from?

617. Who will use or be affected by the result of a Technology Evaluation project?

618. Are others part of the communications management plan?

619. What steps can you take for a positive relationship?

620. In your work, how much time is spent on stakeholder identification?

621. What communications method?

622. What approaches do you use?

623. Why do you manage communications?

624. Who needs to know and how much?

2.31 Risk Management Plan: Technology Evaluation

625. Why do you want risk management?

626. Litigation – what is the probability that lawsuits will cause problems or delays in the Technology Evaluation project?

627. Prioritized components/features?

628. Are the required plans included, such as nonstructural flood risk management plans?

629. What would you do?

630. Could others have been better mitigated?

631. Which risks should get the attention?

632. What is the impact to the Technology Evaluation project if the item is not resolved in a timely fashion?

633. Do the requirements require the creation of components that are unlike anything your organization has previously built?

634. Is security a central objective?

635. Is there anything you would now do differently on your Technology Evaluation project based on this experience?

636. What risks are necessary to achieve success?

637. What are the cost, schedule and resource impacts of avoiding the risk?

638. How is implementation of risk actions performed?

639. What things are likely to change?

640. Do end-users have realistic expectations?

641. Do requirements demand the use of new analysis, design, or testing methods?

642. What did not work so well?

643. How much risk can you tolerate?

2.32 Risk Register: Technology Evaluation

644. Who needs to know about this?

645. Financial risk -can your organization afford to undertake the Technology Evaluation project?

646. When is it going to be done?

647. What are your key risks/show istoppers and what is being done to manage them?

648. Risk categories: what are the main categories of risks that should be addressed on this Technology Evaluation project?

649. How often will the Risk Management Plan and Risk Register be formally reviewed, and by whom?

650. Is further information required before making a decision?

651. Budget and schedule: what are the estimated costs and schedules for performing risk-related activities?

652. Are your objectives at risk?

653. Are there any knock-on effects/impact on any of the other areas?

654. What should the audit role be in establishing a

risk management process?

655. Preventative actions - planned actions to reduce the likelihood a risk will occur and/or reduce the seriousness should it occur. What should you do now?

656. Recovery actions - planned actions taken once a risk has occurred to allow you to move on. What should you do after?

657. Are there any gaps in the evidence?

658. Risk probability and impact: how will the probabilities and impacts of risk items be assessed?

659. Which key risks have ineffective responses or outstanding improvement actions?

660. Manageability – have mitigations to the risk been identified?

661. What further options might be available for responding to the risk?

662. What may happen or not go according to plan?

663. What should you do now?

2.33 Probability and Impact Assessment: Technology Evaluation

664. Risk data quality assessment - what is the quality of the data used to determine or assess the risk?

665. Are people attending meetings and doing work?

666. Risk may be made during which step of risk management?

667. Risks should be identified during which phase of Technology Evaluation project management life cycle?

668. Is it necessary to deeply assess all Technology Evaluation project risks?

669. Risk categorization -which of your categories has more risk than others?

670. Are team members trained in the use of the tools?

671. Who will be in command to monitor and control the performance of the consortium members (consortium leader/client)?

672. Will there be an increase in the political conservatism?

673. Has something like this been done before?

674. Which role do you have in the Technology Evaluation project?

675. Has the need for the Technology Evaluation project been properly established?

676. How do the products attain the specifications?

677. What are the chances the risk event will occur?

678. Sensitivity analysis -which risks will have the most impact on the Technology Evaluation project?

679. Your customers business requirements have suddenly shifted because of a new regulatory statute, what now?

680. Are there alternative opinions/solutions/ processes you should explore?

681. How well is the risk understood?

682. Are some people working on multiple Technology Evaluation projects?

2.34 Probability and Impact Matrix: Technology Evaluation

683. What are the levels of understanding of the future users of this technology?

684. What should be done with risks on the watch list?

685. Mandated specific features?

686. What action would you take to the identified risks in the Technology Evaluation project?

687. Is the technology to be built new to your organization?

688. How would you suggest monitoring for risk transition indicators?

689. How is the risk management process used in practice?

690. Why do you need to manage Technology Evaluation project Risk?

691. Who is going to be the consortium leader?

692. What will be the likely incidence of conflict with neighboring Technology Evaluation projects?

693. Mandated delivery date?

694. Sensitivity analysis -which risks will have the

most impact on the Technology Evaluation project?

695. Can you handle the investment risk?

696. What can possibly go wrong?

697. Do you need a risk management plan?

698. What would be the effect of slippage?

699. How realistic is the timing of introduction?

700. What will be cost of redeployment of the personnel?

701. How do you manage Technology Evaluation project Risk?

702. What is the likelihood?

2.35 Risk Data Sheet: Technology Evaluation

703. Is the data sufficiently specified in terms of the type of failure being analyzed, and its frequency or probability?

704. Who has a vested interest in how you perform as your organization (our stakeholders)?

705. What can happen?

706. What if client refuses?

707. What is the chance that it will happen?

708. What are you here for (Mission)?

709. Do effective diagnostic tests exist?

710. Type of risk identified?

711. What do you know?

712. What actions can be taken to eliminate or remove risk?

713. What are your core values?

714. What do people affected think about the need for, and practicality of preventive measures?

715. Has a sensitivity analysis been carried out?

716. Are new hazards created?

717. How can hazards be reduced?

718. What will be the consequences if it happens?

719. Potential for recurrence?

720. During work activities could hazards exist?

2.36 Procurement Management Plan: Technology Evaluation

721. Is there a formal process for updating the Technology Evaluation project baseline?

722. Are decisions made in a timely manner?

723. Has the budget been baselined?

724. Are Technology Evaluation project team members involved in detailed estimating and scheduling?

725. Were sponsors and decision makers available when needed outside regularly scheduled meetings?

726. Why do you do it?

727. Are corrective actions and variances reported?

728. Have the key functions and capabilities been defined and assigned to each release or iteration?

729. Are the key elements of a Technology Evaluation project Charter present?

730. Measurable - are the targets measurable?

731. What were things that you did very well and want to do the same again on the next Technology Evaluation project?

732. Is there general agreement & acceptance of the current status and progress of the Technology Evaluation project?

733. Are all key components of a Quality Assurance Plan present?

734. Are there checklists created to determine if all quality processes are followed?

735. How will you coordinate Procurement with aspects of the Technology Evaluation project?

736. Are the payment terms being followed?

2.37 Source Selection Criteria: Technology Evaluation

737. What is cost analysis and when should it be performed?

738. How do you facilitate evaluation against published criteria?

739. Can you identify proposed teaming partners and/or subcontractors and consider the nature and extent of proposed involvement in satisfying the Technology Evaluation project requirements?

740. How should oral presentations be evaluated?

741. Who must be notified?

742. Why promote competition?

743. How do you encourage efficiency and consistency?

744. What should a DRFP include?

745. Can you reasonably estimate total organization requirements for the coming year?

746. How long will it take for the purchase cost to be the same as the lease cost?

747. What are the guiding principles for developing an evaluation report?

748. How will you decide an evaluators write up is sufficient?

749. If the costs are normalized, please account for how the normalization is conducted. Is a cost realism analysis used?

750. How organization are proposed quotes/prices?

751. What aspects should the contracting officer brief the Technology Evaluation project on prior to evaluation of proposals?

752. How much past performance information should be requested?

753. How can business terms and conditions be improved to yield more effective price competition?

754. What does an evaluation address and what does a sample resemble?

755. What past performance information should be requested?

756. What documentation is needed for a tradeoff decision?

2.38 Stakeholder Management Plan: Technology Evaluation

757. Are Technology Evaluation project team members committed fulltime?

758. Are actuals compared against estimates to analyze and correct variances?

759. Will the current technology alter during the life of the Technology Evaluation project?

760. Is the steering committee active in Technology Evaluation project oversight?

761. Which of the records created within the Technology Evaluation project, if any, does the Business Owner require access to?

762. How will the equipment be verified?

763. Are stakeholders aware and supportive of the principles and practices of modern software estimation?

764. Who might be involved in developing a charter?

765. Are the schedule estimates reasonable given the Technology Evaluation project?

766. Have all involved stakeholders and work groups committed to the Technology Evaluation project?

767. Are Technology Evaluation project contact logs kept up to date?

768. Are risk oriented checklists used during risk identification?

769. What are the procedures and processes to be followed for purchases, including approval and authorisation requirements?

770. Is pert / critical path or equivalent methodology being used?

771. Has the business need been clearly defined?

772. Who is gathering information?

2.39 Change Management Plan: Technology Evaluation

773. What new behaviours are required?

774. Clearly articulate the overall business benefits of the Technology Evaluation project -why are you doing this now?

775. What processes are in place to manage knowledge about the Technology Evaluation project?

776. Will the culture embrace or reject this change?

777. Who will be the change levers?

778. Why is the initiative is being undertaken - What are the business drivers?

779. What are the responsibilities assigned to each role?

780. What are the major changes to processes?

781. How will you deal with anger about the restricting of communications due to confidentiality considerations?

782. Will a different work structure focus people on what is important?

783. Are work location changes required?

784. Have the systems been configured and tested?

785. What will be the preferred method of delivery?

786. When does it make sense to customize?

787. Have the business unit contacts been briefed by the Technology Evaluation project team?

788. How prevalent is Resistance to Change?

789. Who might be able to help you the most?

790. What time commitment will this involve?

3.0 Executing Process Group: Technology Evaluation

791. How does Technology Evaluation project management relate to other disciplines?

792. Mitigate. what will you do to minimize the impact should a risk event occur?

793. Does the case present a realistic scenario?

794. What business situation is being addressed?

795. Do your results resemble a normal distribution?

796. What Technology Evaluation projects and services are in the portfolio of your organization?

797. What were things that you need to improve?

798. Is the schedule for the set products being met?

799. What are the main types of goods and services being outsourced?

800. What is involved in the solicitation process?

801. Based on your Technology Evaluation project communication management plan, what worked well?

802. Will outside resources be needed to help?

803. How well did the chosen processes produce the expected results?

804. How will you avoid scope creep?

805. Who will provide training?

806. After how many days will the lease cost be the same as the purchase cost for the equipment?

807. What is the shortest possible time it will take to complete this Technology Evaluation project?

3.1 Team Member Status Report: Technology Evaluation

808. Are your organizations Technology Evaluation projects more successful over time?

809. Are the attitudes of staff regarding Technology Evaluation project work improving?

810. How it is to be done?

811. Does the product, good, or service already exist within your organization?

812. How does this product, good, or service meet the needs of the Technology Evaluation project and your organization as a whole?

813. What specific interest groups do you have in place?

814. Is there evidence that staff is taking a more professional approach toward management of your organizations Technology Evaluation projects?

815. Are the products of your organizations Technology Evaluation projects meeting customers objectives?

816. Does every department have to have a Technology Evaluation project Manager on staff?

817. How will resource planning be done?

818. How can you make it practical?

819. The problem with Reward & Recognition Programs is that the truly deserving people all too often get left out. How can you make it practical?

820. When a teams productivity and success depend on collaboration and the efficient flow of information, what generally fails them?

821. Will the staff do training or is that done by a third party?

822. What is to be done?

823. Why is it to be done?

824. Does your organization have the means (staff, money, contract, etc.) to produce or to acquire the product, good, or service?

825. Do you have an Enterprise Technology Evaluation project Management Office (EPMO)?

826. How much risk is involved?

3.2 Change Request: Technology Evaluation

827. Why control change across the life cycle?

828. How do team members communicate with each other?

829. Will this change conflict with other requirements changes (e.g., lead to conflicting operational scenarios)?

830. How do you get changes (code) out in a timely manner?

831. Should staff call into the helpdesk or go to the website?

832. Who is responsible for the implementation and monitoring of all measures?

833. Has your address changed?

834. Is it feasible to use requirements attributes as predictors of reliability?

835. What are the basic mechanics of the Change Advisory Board (CAB)?

836. Who can suggest changes?

837. How are changes requested (forms, method of communication)?

838. How are changes graded and who is responsible for the rating?

839. Where do changes come from?

840. How can you ensure that changes have been made properly?

841. Have all related configuration items been properly updated?

842. Will the change use memory to the extent that other functions will be not have sufficient memory to operate effectively?

843. Will there be a change request form in use?

844. How many lines of code must be changed to implement the change?

845. Will new change requests be acknowledged in a timely manner?

846. Should a more thorough impact analysis be conducted?

3.3 Change Log: Technology Evaluation

847. Is the change backward compatible without limitations?

848. When was the request submitted?

849. Does the suggested change request represent a desired enhancement to the products functionality?

850. How does this relate to the standards developed for specific business processes?

851. Does the suggested change request seem to represent a necessary enhancement to the product?

852. How does this change affect the timeline of the schedule?

853. Do the described changes impact on the integrity or security of the system?

854. Will the Technology Evaluation project fail if the change request is not executed?

855. Is the change request within Technology Evaluation project scope?

856. Is the submitted change a new change or a modification of a previously approved change?

857. Is this a mandatory replacement?

858. Is the change request open, closed or pending?

859. How does this change affect scope?

860. When was the request approved?

861. Is the requested change request a result of changes in other Technology Evaluation project(s)?

862. Who initiated the change request?

3.4 Decision Log: Technology Evaluation

863. At what point in time does loss become unacceptable?

864. How does provision of information, both in terms of content and presentation, influence acceptance of alternative strategies?

865. How does an increasing emphasis on cost containment influence the strategies and tactics used?

866. Which variables make a critical difference?

867. Does anything need to be adjusted?

868. How consolidated and comprehensive a story can you tell by capturing currently available incident data in a central location and through a log of key decisions during an incident?

869. What makes you different or better than others companies selling the same thing?

870. How do you know when you are achieving it?

871. What alternatives/risks were considered?

872. Who will be given a copy of this document and where will it be kept?

873. What are the cost implications?

874. What was the rationale for the decision?

875. Linked to original objective?

876. Who is the decisionmaker?

877. Decision-making process; how will the team make decisions?

878. Do strategies and tactics aimed at less than full control reduce the costs of management or simply shift the cost burden?

879. What is the line where eDiscovery ends and document review begins?

880. With whom was the decision shared or considered?

881. Is your opponent open to a non-traditional workflow, or will it likely challenge anything you do?

882. How does the use a Decision Support System influence the strategies/tactics or costs?

3.5 Quality Audit: Technology Evaluation

883. Has a written procedure been established to identify devices during all stages of receipt, reconditioning, distribution and installation so that mix-ups are prevented?

884. Is the process of self review, learning and improvement endemic throughout your organization?

885. Are there sufficient personnel having the necessary education, background, training, and experience to assure that all operations are correctly performed?

886. How does your organization know that its research programs are appropriately effective and constructive?

887. How does your organization know that its information technology system is serving its needs as effectively and constructively as is appropriate?

888. What is the collective experience of the team to be assigned to an audit?

889. How does your organization know that its management of its ethical responsibilities is appropriately effective and constructive?

890. How does your organization know that the

support for its staff is appropriately effective and constructive?

891. How does your organization know that its system for staff performance planning and review is appropriately effective and constructive?

892. How does your organization know that the research supervision provided to its staff is appropriately effective and constructive?

893. Is there a written corporate quality policy?

894. How does your organization know that its risk management system is appropriately effective and constructive?

895. Do all staff have the necessary authority and resources to deliver what is expected of them?

896. It is inappropriate to seek information about the Audit Panels preliminary views including questions like why do you ask that?

897. What mechanisms exist for identification of staff development needs?

898. What review processes are in place for your organizations major activities?

899. Is there any content that may be legally actionable?

900. What is your organizations greatest strength?

901. How are you auditing your organizations

compliance with regulations?

902. What does an analysis of your organizations staff profile suggest in terms of its planning, and how is this being addressed?

3.6 Team Directory: Technology Evaluation

903. Who should receive information (all stakeholders)?

904. Who are the Team Members?

905. How will you accomplish and manage the objectives?

906. Process decisions: are there any statutory or regulatory issues relevant to the timely execution of work?

907. Does a Technology Evaluation project team directory list all resources assigned to the Technology Evaluation project?

908. Where should the information be distributed?

909. Process decisions: are all start-up, turn over and close out requirements of the contract satisfied?

910. Process decisions: how well was task order work performed?

911. Who will write the meeting minutes and distribute?

912. Who will talk to the customer?

913. Who will be the stakeholders on your next

Technology Evaluation project?

914. Is construction on schedule?

915. Process decisions: do invoice amounts match accepted work in place?

916. Timing: when do the effects of communication take place?

917. What are you going to deliver or accomplish?

918. Why is the work necessary?

919. Process decisions: which organizational elements and which individuals will be assigned management functions?

920. Process decisions: do job conditions warrant additional actions to collect job information and document on-site activity?

921. Decisions: is the most suitable form of contract being used?

922. Do purchase specifications and configurations match requirements?

3.7 Team Operating Agreement: Technology Evaluation

923. Did you delegate tasks such as taking meeting minutes, presenting a topic and soliciting input?

924. Do you brief absent members after they view meeting notes or listen to a recording?

925. Do you vary your voice pace, tone and pitch to engage participants and gain involvement?

926. What are the current caseload numbers in the unit?

927. Are there differences in access to communication and collaboration technology based on team member location?

928. Do you call or email participants to ensure understanding, follow-through and commitment to the meeting outcomes?

929. What are the safety issues/risks that need to be addressed and/or that the team needs to consider?

930. The method to be used in the decision making process; Will it be consensus, majority rule, or the supervisor having the final say?

931. Does your team need access to all documents and information at all times?

932. What is the anticipated procedure (recruitment, solicitation of volunteers, or assignment) for selecting team members?

933. How will your group handle planned absences?

934. Communication protocols: how will the team communicate?

935. What are the boundaries (organizational or geographic) within which you operate?

936. Resource allocation: how will individual team members account for time and expenses, and how will this be allocated in the team budget?

937. Do you ask participants to close laptops and place mobile devices on silent on the table while the meeting is in progress?

938. Do you post meeting notes and the recording (if used) and notify participants?

939. Are team roles clearly defined and accepted?

940. How will group handle unplanned absences?

941. How will you resolve conflict efficiently and respectfully?

942. Do you listen for voice tone and word choice to understand the meaning behind words?

3.8 Team Performance Assessment: Technology Evaluation

943. To what degree are the members clear on what they are individually responsible for and what they are jointly responsible for?

944. To what degree can team members vigorously define the teams purpose in considerations with others who are not part of the functioning team?

945. What makes opportunities more or less obvious?

946. To what degree can team members meet frequently enough to accomplish the teams ends?

947. To what degree does the teams purpose constitute a broader, deeper aspiration than just accomplishing short-term goals?

948. To what degree do team members agree with the goals, relative importance, and the ways in which achievement will be measured?

949. What are you doing specifically to develop the leaders around you?

950. When a reviewer complains about method variance, what is the essence of the complaint?

951. To what degree are sub-teams possible or necessary?

952. To what degree do members articulate the goals beyond the team membership?

953. To what degree are fresh input and perspectives systematically caught and added (for example, through information and analysis, new members, and senior sponsors)?

954. Effects of crew composition on crew performance: Does the whole equal the sum of its parts?

955. To what degree will the team ensure that all members equitably share the work essential to the success of the team?

956. To what degree can all members engage in open and interactive considerations?

957. To what degree does the teams work approach provide opportunity for members to engage in results-based evaluation?

958. Individual task proficiency and team process behavior: what is important for team functioning?

959. When does the medium matter?

960. To what degree do all members feel responsible for all agreed-upon measures?

961. To what degree are the skill areas critical to team performance present?

962. How do you keep key people outside the group informed about its accomplishments?

3.9 Team Member Performance Assessment: Technology Evaluation

963. How do you use data to inform instruction and improve staff achievement?

964. What are the key duties or tasks of the Ratee?

965. What are the staffs preferences for training on technology-based platforms?

966. What is a significant fact or event?

967. How is your organizations Strategic Management System tied to performance measurement?

968. Who should attend?

969. To what extent are systems and applications (e.g., game engine, mobile device platform) utilized?

970. Who they are?

971. Where can team members go for more detailed information on performance measurement and assessment?

972. To what degree are the goals ambitious?

973. Are the goals SMART ?

974. How often are assessments to be conducted?

975. What instructional strategies were developed/incorporated (e.g., direct instruction, indirect instruction, experiential learning, independent study, interactive instruction)?

976. To what degree do team members frequently explore the teams purpose and its implications?

977. To what degree does the team possess adequate membership to achieve its ends?

978. How do you currently use the time that is available?

979. What is the target group for instruction (e.g., individual and collective or small team instruction)?

3.10 Issue Log: Technology Evaluation

980. How do you manage communications?

981. What steps can you take for positive relationships?

982. Where do team members get information?

983. Are there potential barriers between the team and the stakeholder?

984. What is a Stakeholder?

985. What is the impact on the Business Case?

986. What is the status of the issue?

987. Is access to the Issue Log controlled?

988. Why not more evaluators?

989. What effort will a change need?

990. Do you feel more overwhelmed by stakeholders?

991. What does the stakeholder need from the team?

992. What is the stakeholders level of authority?

993. Who are the members of the governing body?

994. Can an impact cause deviation beyond team, stage or Technology Evaluation project tolerances?

995. What approaches to you feel are the best ones to use?

4.0 Monitoring and Controlling Process Group: Technology Evaluation

996. What is the expected monetary value of the Technology Evaluation project?

997. Who are the Technology Evaluation project stakeholders?

998. Who needs to be involved in the planning?

999. How many more potential communications channels were introduced by the discovery of the new stakeholders?

1000. Do the products created live up to the necessary quality?

1001. How to ensure validity, quality and consistency?

1002. What factors are contributing to progress or delay in the achievement of products and results?

1003. What kinds of things in particular are you looking for data on?

1004. Are there areas that need improvement?

1005. How many potential communications channels exist on the Technology Evaluation project?

1006. What are the goals of the program?

1007. What areas were overlooked on this Technology Evaluation project?

1008. What resources are necessary?

1009. How well did the team follow the chosen processes?

1010. What is the timeline?

1011. What good practices or successful experiences or transferable examples have been identified?

4.1 Project Performance Report: Technology Evaluation

1012. To what degree can the cognitive capacity of individuals accommodate the flow of information?

1013. To what degree can the team ensure that all members are individually and jointly accountable for the teams purpose, goals, approach, and work-products?

1014. Next Steps?

1015. To what degree will each member have the opportunity to advance his or her professional skills in all three of the above categories while contributing to the accomplishment of the teams purpose and goals?

1016. What is the PRS?

1017. To what degree are the teams goals and objectives clear, simple, and measurable?

1018. To what degree do the goals specify concrete team work products?

1019. To what degree is the information network consistent with the structure of the formal organization?

1020. To what degree do the relationships of the informal organization motivate taskrelevant behavior and facilitate task completion?

1021. To what degree does the informal organization make use of individual resources and meet individual needs?

1022. To what degree do team members articulate the teams work approach?

1023. What is in it for you?

1024. To what degree is there centralized control of information sharing?

1025. To what degree will the team adopt a concrete, clearly understood, and agreed-upon approach that will result in achievement of the teams goals?

4.2 Variance Analysis: Technology Evaluation

1026. What business event caused the fluctuation?

1027. Did a new competitor enter the market?

1028. Does the scheduling system identify in a timely manner the status of work?

1029. Are management actions taken to reduce indirect costs when there are significant adverse variances?

1030. Historical experience?

1031. Is work properly classified as measured effort, LOE, or apportioned effort and appropriately separated?

1032. Are work packages assigned to performing organizations?

1033. Why do variances exist?

1034. What does a favorable labor efficiency variance mean?

1035. Who are responsible for overhead performance control of related costs?

1036. Who is generally responsible for monitoring and taking action on variances?

1037. Is budgeted cost for work performed calculated in a manner consistent with the way work is planned?

1038. Are all elements of indirect expense identified to overhead cost budgets of Technology Evaluation projections?

1039. Is the market likely to continue to grow at this rate next year?

1040. How do you verify authorization to proceed with all authorized work?

1041. What is the budgeted cost for work scheduled?

1042. Are there changes in the overhead pool and/or organization structures?

1043. How does the monthly budget compare to the actual experience?

1044. What is the performance to date and material commitment?

4.3 Earned Value Status: Technology Evaluation

1045. How much is it going to cost by the finish?

1046. Earned value can be used in almost any Technology Evaluation project situation and in almost any Technology Evaluation project environment. it may be used on large Technology Evaluation projects, medium sized Technology Evaluation projects, tiny Technology Evaluation projects (in cut-down form), complex and simple Technology Evaluation projects and in any market sector. some people, of course, know all about earned value, they have used it for years - but perhaps not as effectively as they could have?

1047. What is the unit of forecast value?

1048. Where are your problem areas?

1049. Validation is a process of ensuring that the developed system will actually achieve the stakeholders desired outcomes; Are you building the right product? What do you validate?

1050. If earned value management (EVM) is so good in determining the true status of a Technology Evaluation project and Technology Evaluation project its completion, why is it that hardly any one uses it in information systems related Technology Evaluation projects?

1051. Are you hitting your Technology Evaluation projects targets?

1052. Where is evidence-based earned value in your organization reported?

1053. Verification is a process of ensuring that the developed system satisfies the stakeholders agreements and specifications; Are you building the product right? What do you verify?

1054. When is it going to finish?

1055. How does this compare with other Technology Evaluation projects?

4.4 Risk Audit: Technology Evaluation

1056. How do you govern assets?

1057. Are tools for analysis and design available?

1058. Does your auditor understand your business?

1059. Are your rules, by-laws and practices non-discriminatory?

1060. Do you have an emergency plan?

1061. Risks with Technology Evaluation projects or new initiatives?

1062. Do you have financial policies and procedures in place to guide officers of your organization/treasurer/general members?

1063. Is all expenditure authorised through an identified process?

1064. How are risk appetites expressed?

1065. Does the team have the right mix of skills?

1066. What is the implication of budget constraint on this process?

1067. Is the customer willing to establish rapid communication links with the developer?

1068. Is your organization able to present

documentary evidence in support of compliance?

1069. Will an appropriate standard of care be applied to all involved?

1070. What is the effect of globalisation; is business becoming too complex and can the auditor rely on auditing standards?

1071. Improving fraud detection: do auditors react to abnormal inconsistencies between financial and non-financial measures?

1072. Is Technology Evaluation project scope stable?

1073. Are all managers or operators of the facility or equipment competent or qualified?

1074. How do you compare to other jurisdictions when managing the risk of ....?

1075. What responsibilities for quality, errors, and outcomes have been delegated to staff (or others) without adequate oversight?

4.5 Contractor Status Report: Technology Evaluation

1076. How long have you been using the services?

1077. What process manages the contracts?

1078. Are there contractual transfer concerns?

1079. If applicable; describe your standard schedule for new software version releases. Are new software version releases included in the standard maintenance plan?

1080. Describe how often regular updates are made to the proposed solution. Are corresponding regular updates included in the standard maintenance plan?

1081. What are the minimum and optimal bandwidth requirements for the proposed solution?

1082. What was the final actual cost?

1083. What was the budget or estimated cost for your organizations services?

1084. What is the average response time for answering a support call?

1085. Who can list a Technology Evaluation project as organization experience, your organization or a previous employee of your organization?

1086. What was the overall budget or estimated cost?

1087. What was the actual budget or estimated cost for your organizations services?

1088. How is risk transferred?

4.6 Formal Acceptance: Technology Evaluation

1089. Was the Technology Evaluation project work done on time, within budget, and according to specification?

1090. Who supplies data?

1091. Does it do what client said it would?

1092. How does your team plan to obtain formal acceptance on your Technology Evaluation project?

1093. Does it do what Technology Evaluation project team said it would?

1094. Did the Technology Evaluation project achieve its MOV?

1095. Was the client satisfied with the Technology Evaluation project results?

1096. What are the requirements against which to test, Who will execute?

1097. Do you buy pre-configured systems or build your own configuration?

1098. Was the Technology Evaluation project managed well?

1099. Is formal acceptance of the Technology

Evaluation project product documented and distributed?

1100. Who would use it?

1101. Was the Technology Evaluation project goal achieved?

1102. What is the Acceptance Management Process?

1103. Was business value realized?

1104. General estimate of the costs and times to complete the Technology Evaluation project?

1105. How well did the team follow the methodology?

1106. Was the sponsor/customer satisfied?

1107. What was done right?

1108. Have all comments been addressed?

5.0 Closing Process Group: Technology Evaluation

1109. What were things that you did very well and want to do the same again on the next Technology Evaluation project?

1110. Is the Technology Evaluation project funded?

1111. What were the actual outcomes?

1112. What is the amount of funding and what Technology Evaluation project phases are funded?

1113. Are there funding or time constraints?

1114. Is there a clear cause and effect between the activity and the lesson learned?

1115. What is the Technology Evaluation project name and date of completion?

1116. Specific - is the objective clear in terms of what, how, when, and where the situation will be changed?

1117. Did the Technology Evaluation project team have the right skills?

1118. Were cost budgets met?

1119. How critical is the Technology Evaluation project success to the success of your organization?

1120. What could have been improved?

1121. What areas were overlooked on this Technology Evaluation project?

1122. Did you do what you said you were going to do?

1123. Was the schedule met?

1124. How well did the chosen processes fit the needs of the Technology Evaluation project?

5.1 Procurement Audit: Technology Evaluation

1125. Does the strategy include a policy for identifying and training suitable procurement staff?

1126. Was there reasonable justification for the need of the purchase, namely when made towards the end of the financial year?

1127. Are the rules for automatic payment in computer programs approved by management prior to implementation?

1128. Are travel expenditures monitored to determine that they are in line with other employees and reasonable for the area of travel?

1129. Is a risk evaluation performed?

1130. Do appropriate controls ensure that procurement decisions are not biased by conflicts of interest or corruption?

1131. Is data securely stored?

1132. Is the issuance of purchase orders scheduled so that orders are not issued daily?

1133. Does the contract meet criteria of completeness and consistency?

1134. Are all pre-numbered checks accounted for on a

regular basis?

1135. Are there authorizations on file to support all deductions from payroll checks?

1136. Did you consider and evaluate alternatives, like bundling needs with other departments or grouping supplies in separate lots with different characteristics?

1137. Are petty cash funds operated on an imprest basis?

1138. How are you making the audit trail easy to follow?

1139. Are information gathered to produce knowledge about procured goods and services, prices paid and supplier performance?

1140. Were any additional works or deliveries admissible, without recourse to a new procurement procedure?

1141. How do you deal with budget constrains and assurance needs?

1142. Was the estimated contract value based on realistic and updated prices?

1143. Are there appropriate controls in place to ensure that procurement complies with the relevant legislation?

1144. Are the purchase order forms designed for efficient and simple completion?

5.2 Contract Close-Out: Technology Evaluation

1145. Was the contract type appropriate?

1146. What happens to the recipient of services?

1147. Parties: who is involved?

1148. Was the contract sufficiently clear so as not to result in numerous disputes and misunderstandings?

1149. Have all contracts been completed?

1150. What is capture management?

1151. How does it work?

1152. Has each contract been audited to verify acceptance and delivery?

1153. Are the signers the authorized officials?

1154. Parties: Authorized?

1155. Change in knowledge?

1156. Why Outsource?

1157. Have all contracts been closed?

1158. Change in circumstances?

1159. How is the contracting office notified of the automatic contract close-out?

1160. Have all contract records been included in the Technology Evaluation project archives?

1161. Was the contract complete without requiring numerous changes and revisions?

1162. Have all acceptance criteria been met prior to final payment to contractors?

1163. How/when used ?

1164. Change in attitude or behavior?

5.3 Project or Phase Close-Out: Technology Evaluation

1165. Does the lesson describe a function that would be done differently the next time?

1166. Were risks identified and mitigated?

1167. What could be done to improve the process?

1168. Complete yes or no?

1169. Who controlled key decisions that were made?

1170. Is the lesson significant, valid, and applicable?

1171. What is a Risk?

1172. What stakeholder group needs, expectations, and interests are being met by the Technology Evaluation project?

1173. What process was planned for managing issues/risks?

1174. What was learned?

1175. Have business partners been involved extensively, and what data was required for them?

1176. What information did each stakeholder need to contribute to the Technology Evaluation projects success?

1177. What went well?

1178. Who are the Technology Evaluation project stakeholders and what are roles and involvement?

1179. Were the outcomes different from the already stated planned?

1180. How often did each stakeholder need an update?

1181. What were the desired outcomes?

5.4 Lessons Learned: Technology Evaluation

1182. What is below the surface?

1183. What were the key issues?

1184. How clear were you on your role in the Technology Evaluation project?

1185. What are the influence patterns?

1186. What is the quality and content of communication?

1187. How objective was the collection of data?

1188. How effective was the acceptance management process?

1189. How effectively were issues managed on the Technology Evaluation project?

1190. How well were Technology Evaluation project issues communicated throughout your involvement in the Technology Evaluation project?

1191. How adequately involved did you feel in Technology Evaluation project decisions?

1192. What is the skill mix defined for the staffing?

1193. What were the success factors?

1194. What is your organizations performance history?

1195. How useful was the content of the training you received in preparation for the use of the product/service?

1196. How satisfied are you with your involvement in the development and/or review of the Technology Evaluation project Scope during Technology Evaluation project Initiation and Planning?

1197. How well prepared were you to receive Technology Evaluation project deliverables?

1198. What were the main bottlenecks on the process?

1199. Will the information remain current?

1200. What Technology Evaluation project circumstances were not anticipated?

Index

already   125, 154, 186, 189, 191, 217, 259
Although   129
always 9
ambitious   234
amount   19, 149, 252
amounts   229
amplify60, 116
analysis   2, 6, 9-10, 57, 60, 62-63, 66, 70, 75, 133, 137, 142,
149, 157, 179, 189, 191, 198, 202-203, 205, 209-210, 220, 227, 233,
242, 246
analyze   2, 57, 60, 70, 211
analyzed   93, 129, 175, 205
analyzes   138, 184
another   151
answer 10-11, 15, 26, 42, 57, 73, 89, 102
answered   25, 41, 56, 72, 88, 100, 126
answering   10, 162, 248
anyone   39, 113, 121
anything   159, 166, 175, 197, 223-224
appear   1
appetites   246
applicable   10, 99, 142, 248, 258
applied   81, 99, 154, 161, 247
appointed   31, 35
approach   84, 120, 123, 133, 139, 175, 217, 233, 240-241
approaches   80, 196, 237
approval   30, 108, 141, 212
approvals   141-142
approve   148
approved   35, 71, 129, 146, 181, 185, 221-222, 254
approving   145
Architects   7
archived   176
archives   257
around105, 122, 232
articulate   213, 233, 241
asking 1, 7, 187-188
aspects   162, 208, 210
aspiration   232
assess   27, 74, 113, 164, 184, 201
assessable   170
assessed   82, 194, 200
assessing   85, 93

burden224
business   1, 7, 9, 16, 27, 31, 43-44, 49, 63, 68, 77, 80, 96,
114, 116-117, 121-123, 125, 128-129, 138, 142-143, 189, 202, 210-
215, 221, 236, 242, 246-247, 251, 258
buy-in 107
by-laws   246
calculate   162, 165
calculated   243
cannot165, 174, 178
capability   139
capable   7, 39
capacities   109
capacity   15, 82, 135, 240
capital124
capture   55, 99, 256
captured   53, 85, 111, 139, 175
capturing   223
career 145, 170
careers   104
carried67, 205
caseload   230
categories   199, 201, 240
caught233
caused   1, 52, 242
causes 50-52, 57, 59, 66, 68, 93, 137
causing   25, 149
celebrate   77
center 45, 138
central197, 223
certain169
certified   175
challenge   7, 224
challenges   109, 162
chance   205
chances   202
change   5, 15, 25, 34, 44, 51, 61, 63, 70-71, 75, 82, 84-85,
90, 122, 131-132, 137, 139, 141, 147-148, 151, 160, 165, 174, 176-
177, 181, 183, 187, 193, 198, 213-214, 219-222, 236, 256-257
changed   17, 34, 91, 115, 174, 179, 182, 219-220, 252
changes   23, 26, 32, 37, 46, 71, 77, 79, 95, 100, 103, 113,
123, 129, 143, 148-149, 154, 168, 174, 181, 183, 189, 192, 194,
213, 219-222, 243, 257
changing   91, 105

271

derive 93
describe   16, 145, 162, 248, 258
described   1, 143, 148, 221
describing   41, 170
deserving   218
design 1, 9, 59, 79-80, 98, 123, 149, 198, 246
designed   7, 9, 63, 255
designing   7
desired23, 40, 66, 85, 221, 244, 259
detail   74, 151, 161
detailed   60, 68, 135, 140, 154, 159, 193, 207, 234
details 54
detect 91, 186
detection   247
determine   9, 104, 154, 179, 201, 208, 254
determined   58, 104, 187-188, 194
determines   177
detracting   107
develop   55, 73, 82-83, 86, 137, 151, 232
developed   9, 32, 34-35, 44, 74, 80, 141, 154, 163, 176, 187,
221, 235, 244-245
developer   246
developing   62, 136, 154, 173, 209, 211
deviation   236
device 234
devices   225, 231
diagnostic   205
diagram   3, 46, 59, 164-165, 174
diagrams   45
Dictionary   3, 153
differ   173
difference   167, 223
different   7, 21, 27-28, 34, 59-60, 104, 122, 130, 139, 150,
192-193, 213, 223, 255, 259
difficult61, 160, 163, 169, 176
dilemma   123
dimensions   16
direct   154, 235
direction   34, 46, 137
directly1, 60, 72, 129
Directory   5, 228
Disagree   10, 15, 26, 42, 57, 73, 89, 102
disaster   43, 45, 174

CPSIA information can be obtained
at www.ICGtesting.com
Printed in the USA
BVHW091740270819
556849BV00006B/211/P